The Cryptoterrestrials

Also by Mac Tonnies

After the Martian Apocalypse:
Extraterrestrial Artifacts and the Case for Mars Exploration

Illuminated Black and Other Adventures

The Cryptoterrestrials:
A Meditation on Indigenous Humanoids and the Aliens Among Us

Mac Tonnies

ANOMALIST BOOKS
San Antonio * New York

An Original Publication of ANOMALIST BOOKS

THE CRYPTOTERRESTRIALS

Cover image and design by Nadia Sobin

Illustrations by Mike Clelland

Book design by Seale Studios

For information, go to anomalistbooks.com, or write to:
Anomalist Books, 5150 Broadway #108, San Antonio,
TX 78209

Contents

Editor's Note

Mac Tonnies died in his sleep on the evening of October 18, 2009, at the age of 34. He was weeks away from turning in his manuscript on *The Cryptoterrestrials*. With the help of his family and friends, we have been able to piece together this, his final book.

In particular, I would like to thank:

His mother, Dana Tonnies, for rescuing the hard copy of the manuscript he had left on his desk and had been working on;

David Peeples, for emailing us the digital file of the manuscript that Mac had asked him to print out when his own printer broke down, and for later checking Mac's laptop, with Dana's help, for any more recent versions of the file (there were none);

Nadia Sobin, whose striking artwork graces the cover of his book;

Mike Clelland, who contributed the wonderful interior art;

And to Nick Redfern for the Foreword, and Greg Bishop for the Afterword.

I have lost an author; two have lost a son; thousands have lost a friend; and in the face of intractable mysteries, we have all lost a brilliant thinker.

"Instead of looking at the screen, what I want to do is to turn around and look the other way. When we look the other way what we see is a little hole at the top of the wall with some light coming out. That's where I want to go. I want to steal the key to the projectionist's booth, and then, when everybody has gone home, I want to break in."—Jacques Vallee

"We are part of a symbiotic relationship with something which disguises itself as an extraterrestrial invasion so as not to alarm us."—Terence McKenna

"We're on your street, but you don't see us. Or if you do you smile and say hello."—Morrissey

Foreword

As a result of its elusive, ever-changing and (I would strongly argue) seemingly stage-managed nature and appearance, the UFO phenomenon is one that should be firmly recognized by, and appreciated for, its many attendant uncertainties and complexities.

After all, we should never forget that more than 60 years have elapsed since pilot Kenneth Arnold experienced his now historic encounter of the Flying Saucer kind over Mount Rainier in Washington State. And guess what? The "U" in "UFO" *still* stands for "Unidentified."

Unfortunately, so many of those who have dared to immerse themselves within the ufological sand-pit since that long-gone, heady day in June 1947 have forgotten—or stubbornly refuse to acknowledge—that stark fact.

For those utterly belief-driven souls, the only answer to the ever-present UFO mystery that continues to intrude upon us at a collective and, sometimes, profoundly personal level, is that the true "unknowns" have extraterrestrial origins.

Yet, the harsh reality is that the likes of the late J. Allen Hynek, Leonard Stringfield, Richard Hall, and countless other souls who became entranced by flying saucers and their forever elusive crews were utterly unable to provide any hard evidence that E.T. really was—or still is—among us.

For all their files (and attendant filing cabinets), their carefully compiled notes, and their myriad interviews with numerous eyewitnesses, they failed to make a definitive case. That's right: THEY FAILED. Deal with it or don't, but it's a fact.

Now, one might reasonably ask: well, just because absolute vindication for the Extraterrestrial Hypothesis (ETH) has not yet been forthcoming, does that mean the same hypothesis has no merit?

Of course not; however, in my view, if evidence for the ETH has failed to surface—despite decades of hard work and diligent investigations—then maybe we should consider the notion that we are looking for the answers in all the wrong places.

Instead of looking up, maybe we should be looking around us. And, perhaps, even below us, too.

Thankfully, there are a few learned scholars out there who recognize that what, to some, is a relatively straight-forward matter—namely, the idea that E.T. is visiting us, sometimes crashes and burns, and has a particular penchant for our DNA—is actually nothing of the sort.

Enter Mac Tonnies.

I rather liken Mac to a Fortean equivalent of the Sex Pistols and the Ramones (Mac would probably prefer I cite the Smiths or R.E.M.; but, hey, that's how it goes). When, in 1976, both bands firmly saved rock music from the bloated stodge of groups like Led Zeppelin, Deep Purple, Yes, and Emerson, Lake & Palmer, they didn't do so just because they could. No, their actions were prompted by the fact that (A) the dinosaurs of rock had become utterly irrelevant and redundant; and (B) a new, fresh approach was sorely needed.

Such is the case with the beliefs of many of the long-term players within ufology, who are, today, about as relevant to the actual subject matter as is a pterodactyl or a woolly mammoth to the 21st century.

Even a relative novice cannot fail to notice that the UFO issue has a distinct atmosphere about it that screams "manipulation, deception, and stage-managed trickery." In other words, yes: there is a real UFO phenomenon. And, it has nothing to do with Pentagon generals, CIA spooks, mistaken identity, or outright hoaxing and fakery. But it may have nothing to do with literal extraterrestrials either.

What if there exists alongside us, in distinct stealth, a

race of incredibly ancient beings who may be native to our planet; who were perhaps—eons ago—our technological masters, but who, today, may well be on the wane?

What if, as a means to move amongst us, they have ingeniously passed themselves off as visitors from far-off worlds? And what if we—those of us who delve into the world of the UFO, and those who have encountered such entities—have fallen for their Machiavellian ruses time and time again?

Such are the questions that are at the heart of Mac Tonnies' *The Cryptoterrestrials*.

As Mac skillfully demonstrates, UFOs and their shadowy crews most assuredly do exist, and their ties to us are both long-standing and vital. They *want* us to believe they are extraterrestrials. Arguably, they even *need* us to believe they are extraterrestrials. But, in reality, they are merely Oscar-deserving actors, endlessly performing stage-plays that have successfully kept the human race in the dark for countless generations.

With the long-awaited publication of Mac's *The Cryptoterrestrials*, however, their era of deceit and manipulation may well be coming to a close—providing, that is, we do not continue to be seduced and enchanted by their cosmic lies.

– Nick Redfern

CHAPTER 1

Looking for Aliens

Looking down from a sufficient distance, human habitation recedes to the merest glimmer. As night devours the continents, our seeming dominion vanishes, replaced by scattered constellations, the haughty gleam of our cities suddenly as substantial as a skein of campfires. As the dark deepens, we realize with mounting unease just how tenuous our presence is; the mountains, prairies and lakes, denuded of daylight, taunt us with their enormity.

Then there are the oceans, almost entirely vacant of man-made lights. Our seas, so often taken for granted, are like vast tombs from which even the most unseemly phantasms might emerge; we ply their waters at our own peril, distantly aware that we might find ourselves in the company of others.

The Earth is ancient, its biosphere only slightly less so. For four billion years our world has secreted life. The advent of homo sapiens is alarmingly recent in comparison. We're like foundlings washed upon some alien shore, stifling our fears by pretending to a feeble omnipotence.

Having launched spacecraft to the outer planets and in-spected the crater-pocked wastes of Mars through the unblinking eyes of rovers, it's easy to entertain the idea that we're the first, evolution's sole successful stab at the phenomenon we casually term "intelligence."

Yet as we watch night erode the familiar highways and stadiums and ever-encroaching suburbs, our confi-dence falters. Already, technological forecasters envision a near-future populated by our artificially intelligent off-spring. Perhaps as our most cherished certainties crumble in the glow of a new century—full of danger, portent and enigma—it's become relatively easy to contemplate the presence of the Other; not an other new to our planet, but one predating our own genetic regime. Something unspo-ken and ancient yet nevertheless amenable to science . . . an intelligence with an almost-human face, until recently content to abide by the shadows of our complacency.

But since the middle of the last century it seems to have asserted itself with a vigor hitherto found only in the domain of folklore. Understandably daunted, we've relegated its existence to the margins of perception: hal-lucination, war fever, misunderstood natural phenom-ena, delusion, butchered recollections of dreams best left forgotten. We see lights dancing in our sky and invoke impossible meteors. Landed vehicles accompanied by surreal humanoids become military test aircraft and their diminutive pilots. The emaciated creatures seen aboard apparent spacecraft—or, more portentously, within rock-walled caverns—are summarily dismissed as sheerest fantasy or, at best, as the spawn of novel brain dysfunc-tions.

In the decades since 1947, dawn of the contemporary UFO era, we've confronted a parade of strangeness that has rallied uncritical enthusiasts and rattled entrenched authority, leaving a bizarre residue that defies attempts at categorization as certainly as it elicits hypotheses.

I began this book pursuing the commonalities be-

tween the UFO phenomenon and the equally bewildering spectacle of our emerging technological future. I was
especially intrigued by the prospect of humans becoming something other than strictly biological, increasingly
viewed as a necessary evolutionary step in the wake of
an imminent "Singularity," a moment in history in which
our intelligence, augmented and disseminated by machines, transcends the imaginable.

My working hypothesis—that alien visitation was
best viewed in cybernetic terms—remains a valid paradigm for interpreting the arrival of an alien intelligence
on this planet. But the more I read and contemplated, the
more my "postbiological" theory seemed lacking; while I
could readily envision a global "invasion" directed by an
unseen machine intelligence, the enduring nature of the
UFO spectacle forced me to rethink my assumptions.

Like ufologist Jacques Vallee, I viewed our response
to the appearance of apparent nonhuman vehicles in our
skies as the work of deliberate psychological conditioning (probably, but not necessarily, benevolent). Contrary
to popular perceptions, UFOs are far from a recent occur-
rence; written and oral accounts point to an experience of
exceptional age and patience. If "alien encounters" were
the work of some godlike artificial intelligence, an omniscient pacemaker sowing memes in an effort to ensure
our evolution conformed to some unknown alien ideal,
then we might reasonably expect it to remain "hidden."

This would neatly account for the lack of "hard" evidence that would force the UFO question out of theoretical limbo and into the mainstream. A postbiological
overseer—something along the lines of the inscrutable
black monolith in 2001—would have a vested interest in
obscurity. As biological beings, we might even lack the
perceptual acumen to properly discern its presence. This,
I reasoned, explained the UFO phenomenon's recurrence
in world folklore; perhaps it had succeeded in insinuating itself into our collective unconscious. As abductee

Whitley Strieber has suggested, "alien" contact—whatever "alien" might ultimately mean—might be what the process of evolution looks like to the human mind.

The primary challenge to this mythological approach was the explicitly physical nature of so many encounters—including, but by no means limited to, the relatively recent epidemic of "abductions," in which witnesses report being kidnapped from workaday surroundings and subjected to novel medical tests. This seemed remarkably crude for an intelligence as subtle and abiding as the entity I had imagined. If recent developments in our own technology are any indication at all, we will probably harness much less intrusive techniques within the next few decades; for an intelligence thousands or millions of years superior to our own to stoop to such clinical levels struck me as absurd.

Of course, the very idea of an artificially emplaced psychosocial conditioning system hinges on absurdity. Vallee and John Keel, author of the paranormal masterpiece *The Mothman Prophecies*, have written extensively on the nonsensical element that accompanies so many accounts of assumed extraterrestrial visitation. This absurdity only makes sense if the phenomenon isn't as it seems but rather appeals to our collective unconscious (for reasons we can only guess).

Or so I thought. Finally, I wondered the unthinkable: what if the antics of the "absurd humanoids" documented by Vallee weren't the work of some overarching intelligence? What if they happened just as reported, without the need to invoke externally imposed psychosocial thermostats?

This notion struck me as deliciously ironic. It suggested that the encounters with nonhumans that haunt our folklore were real, not necessarily projections preying on our gullibility. Could "fairies" and "elves"—and all their mythical successors—be distorted representations of an actual species?

While curiously appealing, the idea seemed totally orthogonal to science. Psychologists maintain that legendary "little people" are beings of the mind, the brain's instinctive attempt to populate the darkness. They're also quick to point out that modern accounts of spindly gray aliens are almost certainly due to fantasy-prone personalities, poorly trained therapists, and hallucinations experienced during episodes of sleep paralysis.

This analysis is attractive on several levels. It neatly does away with the specter of the Other we repeatedly encounter in myths. It also assuages our fears that our world might be fair game for dispassionate ET scientists, with their glittering probes and omnipotent saucers.

Alas, it fails.

This book documents a most unconventional slant on the enduring UFO mystery. In *The Cryptoterrestrials*, I attempt to reconcile mythological and contemporary accounts of "little people" into a coherent picture. In many ways, the image that emerges is at least as frightening as my original cybernetic premise: it's much closer to home, vastly less abstract, and—tantalizingly—amenable to scientific testing.

I propose that at least some accounts of alien visitation can be attributed to a humanoid species indigenous to the Earth, a sister race that has adapted to our numerical superiority by developing a surprisingly robust technology. The explicitly reproductive overtones that color many encounters suggest that these "indigenous aliens" are imperiled by a malady that has gone uncured throughout the eons we have coexisted. Driven by a puzzling mixture of hubris and existential desperation, they seek to perpetuate themselves by infusing their gene-pool with human DNA. While existing at the very margins of ordinary human perception, they have succeeded in realms practically unexplored by known terrestrial science, reinventing themselves at will and helping to orchestrate a misinformation campaign of awe-inspiring scope.

Is the intelligence behind the close-encounter experience using science-fictional devices as a way of interacting with us, much how a primatologist "communicates" with an orphaned monkey via hand-puppet? If so, how to account for descriptions of bug-like entities from populations who haven't been primed to know what an alien "should" look like? Maybe the ubiquitous "Gray" is simply a costume that works, in which case one can't help but yearn for a glimpse of next year's fashions . . .

For too long, we've called them "aliens," assuming that we represent our planet's best and brightest.

Maybe that's exactly what they want us to think.

CHAPTER 2

Misdirection

Every few nights I get out my laser pointer and indulge my cats in a frenetic game of "chase." Cats are natural hunters, and they're effectively incapable of not looking at the quickly moving red dot that I project onto the carpet, walls, or any piece of furniture that happens to be in its path.

To my cats, the red dot possesses its own vitality. It exists as a distinct entity. While they may see me holding the pointer, they can't (or won't) be distracted by such things once the button is pressed and the living room is suddenly alive with luminous vermin. So they chase it. And, if they get close enough, even take swipes at it—I make the dot "flee" or disappear in what seems like a concession of defeat (which, of course, only further arouses the cats' predatory curiosity).

All the while I'm controlling the red dot, I'm taking pains to make it behave like something intelligible. Just waving the pointer around the room wouldn't be any fun. So I make it "climb," "jump," and scuttle when cornered, even though the laser's impervious to obstructions.

This sense of physicality seems to be the element that makes chasing the laser so engaging—both for the cats and for me.

I can't help but be reminded of our continuing search for assumed extraterrestrial vehicles. UFO sightings demonstrate many of the same aspects of a typical feline laser hunt: mysterious disappearances, "impossible" maneuvers, and a predilection for trickery—the apparent *desire* to be seen despite (or because of) a technology presumed to be far in advance of our own. More than one UFO researcher has noted that UFOs behave more like projections or holograms than nuts-and-bolts craft . . . an observation that begs the nature of the intelligence doing the projecting.

According to astrophysicist Vallee, UFOs are part of a psychosocial conditioning system by which perceived "rewards" are doled out to reconcile for the dearth of irrefutable physical evidence. The phenomenon—whatever its ultimate nature—obstinately *denies itself*, thus enabling the very game it's intent on playing with us.

We see that sudden spark of red light; we pounce. *This* time we'll catch it for sure.

My interest in UFOs crystallized in elementary school upon the discovery of Gary Kinder's *Light Years*, an account of the alleged contacts of Swiss cultist Billy Meier. I wasn't entirely sold by Kinder's book, but my interest was piqued (even though the emphatically human-looking extraterrestrials described by Meier troubled me on some unspoken level).

Later encounters with books about exobiology only made Meier's stories sound all the more absurd. Not only did I find the commonly depicted "Grays" more convincingly alien, I considered the body of "abductee" literature infinitely more compelling than tales of sage galactic emissaries. Even if most accounts of "bedroom visitations" could be explained in terms of sleep paralysis, there seemed to be a genuine signal embedded in the pop-cultural noise.

Throughout high school and college I refined my study of UFO-themed literature and came away thoroughly disillusioned—but oddly invigorated. Classic narratives such as John Fuller's *The Interrupted Journey* and Jacques Vallee's *Dimensions*—an expanded version of his seminal mythological analysis *Passport to Magonia*—convinced me that the "believers" had it wrong, as did the majority of self-proclaimed skeptics.

I've since waded through hundreds of books about the alleged alien presence on our planet and come away largely convinced that we're sharing our world with an advanced form of intelligence. While not necessarily extraterrestrial, this intelligence is certainly not human in any normal sense. Yet it interacts with us in a manner that, at times, seems comprehensible—which isn't what one would expect of dispassionate observers or mere extraterrestrial anthropologists.

That we've seen traces of its existence at all alludes to either its technological fallibility or its concerted *desire* to be seen. Both possibilities are disturbing from conventional exobiological and ufological perspectives. The aliens—whatever they are—aren't simply visiting. They've quietly taken up residence.

The more I researched the history and morphology of "alien" contact, the more I became convinced the reigning Extraterrestrial Hypothesis (ETH) was profoundly lacking. But even the most lucid opponents of the ETH, aside from offering vague (albeit endlessly enticing) references to "other dimensions" and "parallel universes," seemed dumbstruck by the phenomenon's absurdity; I had yet to read of a plausible means by which the "aliens'" home world could intersect our own, allowing a steady stream of ufonauts.

We typically assume interdimensional travel must involve arcane cosmological machinery such as a wormhole or "stargate." But I became increasingly drawn to the idea that our visitors' method of travel is less flashy (from a technical perspective) and more understandable in terms of earthly—if bizarre—paranormal influences.

This led to my growing suspicion that the "aliens" typically attributed to extrasolar planets are less advanced than they lead us to believe. In fact, I think a case can be made that we're dealing with a surprisingly vulnerable intelligence that relies largely on subterfuge and disinformation to achieve its goals, a theme I attempt to address in later chapters.

And as outlandish as it may seem, I've been forced to wrestle with the notion that our relationship with these "others" is far more widespread and intimate than even paranoid dramatizations of the UFO spectacle would have us believe.

These dawning suspicions are borne out, at least in part, by world folklore (with its preoccupation with "little people" in our midst) as well as by recent discoveries that suggest the history of our species is more enigmatic than we'd like to admit. We may well share our planet with cryptohominids that have mastered the art of camouflage in order to coexist with us. More portentously, their agenda might be within our ability to grasp. But to do so, we must suspend the assumption that we're dealing with something as quaint as ET astronauts.

The truth, unnervingly, seems much closer to home, threatening to displace our sense of self in a most unexpected manner.

I sometimes see my name used in conjunction with the word "ufology." Loosely defined, ufology is the study

of the UFO phenomenon. This includes disciplines ranging from metallurgy to psychology, from neuroanatomy
to string theory. The best UFO literature benefits from the
reasoned inclusion of as many perspectives as possible,
even those that would seem to refute the very phenomenon under investigation. (The pronounced lack of such
books is predominantly why it's fashionable for intel-
lectuals to adopt a scoffing, can't-be-bothered approach
when addressing UFOs—a most intriguing reaction,
given that "UFO" simply denotes an aerial object of unknown origin.)

Am I a ufologist? I don't know. Maybe. If I am, I
should probably qualify the "U" word with "theoretical."
There are theoretical physicists and literary theorists;
why not theoretical ufologists?

The ufological "community" suffers from creative
anemia. It has a disheartening tendency to refute dissent-
ing voices—even those within its own ranks—with tired
screeds that unnecessarily polarize the debate (such as
it is) between cautious advocates of the Extraterrestrial
Hypothesis and know-nothing science popularizers who
seem genuinely incapable of considering the UFO inquiry
outside the cognitive barriers posed by decades of cheesy
sci-fi cinema and the legacy of myriad True Believers.

So it's no real surprise why ufology is marginal. While
its luminaries might noisily claim otherwise, ufology collectively *wants* to be marginal. With the lamentable excep-
tion of a few spokesmen who feel the need to "explain"
the phenomenon's intricacies to a wary public (often in
the guise of would-be political discourse), the ostensible
UFO community remains afraid of stepping into the rude
glow of widespread public attention.

And it has a right to be be afraid. Having dotingly
constructed a theoretical house of straw, many ufological proponents secretly prefer the tenuous camaraderie
of their peers to the much more exciting prospect of being taken seriously by science. (This isn't to condemn

UFO research as anti-scientific; perhaps the only reason the field remains afloat at all is the pioneering effort of scientists such as James McDonald, J. Allen Hynek, and Jacques Vallee.)

But the era of genuine hypotheses seems to be nearing an end. The "old guard," inexplicably enamored of the Extraterrestrial Hypothesis, is now engaged in little more than ideological turf-wars. The boons of speculation have been quietly set aside in favor of models that make just enough sense to allow their defenders to issue brittle proclamations with semi-straight faces.

Meanwhile, the enigma persists—as always, seemingly just beyond our comprehension. And we have the nerve to wonder why.

CHAPTER 3

UFOs and the ETH

What do we know about the UFO phenomenon? What can researchers agree on, if anything? I certainly don't expect them to hop on the cryptoterrestrial bandwagon. Neither do I expect ufologists to agree on the ever-nebulous Interdimensional Hypothesis, which raises at least as many reality-altering questions as it purports to answer.

At the same time, the Null Hypothesis, maintaining that UFOs can be universally ascribed to misidentified natural phenomena and sightings of unconventional earthly aircraft, has grown decrepit and toothless. Fashionable debunking aside (up to and including the brittle posturing of self-styled "alien experts" such as the SETI Institute's Seth Shostak), something absolutely fascinating is happening.

Taking stock of the situation, I'm tempted to reduce the UFO riddle to a few guiding tenets which I think can be reasonably supported by the evidence provided since the "modern" era of sightings began more than 60 years ago. A list of pertinent characteristics might go like this:

1.) Regardless of their origin, UFOs are physically real.

2.) UFOs are sometimes observed engaged in behavior which can only be described as intelligently directed.

3.) The psychological and sociological impact of the phenomenon is especially enduring and should be a topic of paramount interest for scholars and researchers in fields as disparate as cultural anthropology, aeronautics, and neurology.

4.) The sometimes theatrical behavior of unidentified flying objects suggests the possibility of some form of dialogue, whether directed by ourselves or orchestrated by the phenomenon itself. Likewise, certain military encounters in which weapons systems have been apparently manipulated in intelligent fashion invite the prospect that the UFO intelligence is at least partially amenable to understanding in terms of human psychology.

If the UFO intelligence is indigenous to this planet, then the pronounced extraterrestrial flavor of so many of our most hallowed (if controversial) beliefs may be an attempt to convince us the answer to the UFO riddle lies somewhere in the stars.

So we gaze upward in wonder and fear while the phenomenon continues—unabated and overlooked.

UFOs cruise our skies with an implacable arrogance. If our visitors are indeed extrasolar aliens, then they have a most curious penchant for drama. If, on the other hand, we're observing the activities of a cryptoterrestrial civilization, the apparent desire to be seen can be readily explained in terms of misdirection.

"Alien" imagery is the perfect cover, as our own military understands all-too-well. Greg Bishop chronicles just one example in *Project Beta*, a devastating critique of the

black-ops underworld and its readiness to exploit ET mythology in order to deflate serious interest in secret Air
Force projects.

By utilizing our innate fascination with interplane-
tary visitors, the cryptoterrestrials have ensured that any
accidental sightings of their craft will be ascribed to the
ETH. The mainstream media, quick to "debunk" for fear
of inciting ridicule, thus ignores credible sightings and inadvertently assists the cryptoterrestrial agenda. And if by
some chance the sighting is undeniable, its cultural con-
notations will almost certainly relegate it to our collective
fortean attic.

In a related vein, I don't think it's accidental that
so many UFOs are adorned with mesmerizing flashing
lights. While one can always argue that conspicuous
lights indicate the presence of some truly unearthly propulsion system, it's just as possible that they're a deliberate (and relatively low-tech) attempt to make a rather
ordinary conveyance look unearthly, thereby eliciting the
excitement of the very ET enthusiasts whose sightings are
certain to be ignored . . . or, at best, published in some
obscure journal or website.

As Vallee has astutely noted, many accounts of UFO
landings have the undeniable flavor of staged events.
The controversial events at Rendlesham, for instance,
seem to make sense only if they were intended to be witnessed, perhaps in an attempt to further impress us with
the extraterrestrial meme. In the same vein, the famous
Washington National sightings of 1952, in which objects
were tracked over Washington, D.C. with ground-and
air-based radar and confirmed visually by multiple witnesses, smack of an orchestrated event intended to arrest
our attention.

Intriguingly, the objects over Washington were limited to inexplicable sources of light—not the "structured
craft" described in other notable cases. Could the UFO
intelligence use a form of holography to trick us into

thinking we're observing tangible vehicles? The possibility can't be discounted. Michael Talbot supports the holographic theory in his book *The Holographic Universe*, noting that some UFO displays have more in common with sophisticated projections than spacecraft.

The same can be said of many close encounters of the third or fourth kind in which witnesses report anomalous spatial effects. Some witnesses have described the interior of apparent alien vehicles as considerably larger than the craft as seen from outside; this odd detail, so bizarre when considered in isolation, might be explained as a perceptual trick enacted by the "aliens" to render their vehicles more impressive than they actually are. Upon exiting, a witness would be more likely to describe the experience in otherworldly terms.

The UFO debate has become undeniably polarized, especially in the United States. Jacques Vallee has attributed the fixation with the Extraterrestrial Hypothesis to the urge to "kick the tires," which seems to suggest that Americans are skeptical of alien visitation. Rather paradoxically, polls show that Americans' acceptance of alien visitors in nuts-and-bolts spacecraft is alive and even thriving, with the end of the 20th century's rash of abduction reports fueling belief in both ETs and a probable government cover-up.

This predisposition to address the UFO enigma in predominantly "aerospace" terms has starved objective research by alienating mainstream scientists (bored with unsubstantiated tales of close encounters or odd lights in the sky) by implying the phenomenon is necessarily physical. If physical, argue debunkers, the alien presence should be self-evident, especially in our era of automated surveillance.

Equally lamentable, little or no effort is expended trying to fathom the psychology of ETs. SETI, for instance, remains largely a technological effort, with hypothetical aliens governed by the same conceits and prejudices that influence the field's guiding researchers.

This casual anthropomorphism undermines the mainstream's dealings with ET intelligence. Needless to say, it completely bypasses the idea that some form of nonhuman intelligence may already be in our midst. If nonhumans are in fact at our doorstep, it stands to reason that they would exploit our predilection for "space aliens." If they possess a technology even slightly more advanced than ours, staging "extraterrestrial" landings may prove irresistible.

But the extraterrestrial bias is even more damaging in scope. Its assumption that the cosmos will inevitably yield its secrets to our ever-improving instrumental capability lures us from other, equally enticing, models of reality that may have much more bearing on the prospect of nonhuman life and consciousness. Shamans of so-called "primitive" cultures have long relied on altered states to communicate with otherworldly intelligences. Psychedelic drugs commonly facilitate or heighten this communication, implying a deep-rooted neurological mechanism. The various altered states described by "abductees" suggest a common origin, allowing the possibility that "others" might exploit mind-to-mind communication as casually as we use cellphones and broadband internet.

If a shadow race of earthly humanoids has achieved some form of telepathy, we may be well on the way to bridging the gulf. Powerful computers have already been set to work simulating the interactions that define "thought" on the sub-cellular level. Electron microscopy has revealed "protein microtubules" thought to make use of quantum effects. British mathematician Roger Penrose, an early collaborator with Stephen Hawking, has claimed

31

that our brains' quantum nature prohibits the construction of artificial minds—the stated aim of artificial intelligence research. Although the verdict certainly isn't in—and may not be until scientists unravel the mind-brain dichotomy—it's interesting to note the role of parallel universes in a world governed by quantum mechanics.

Physicist David Deutsch, for instance, advocates the still-controversial Many Worlds Interpretation (MWI) of quantum theory, in which our universe bifurcates each time a subatomic event's wave function "collapses." Taken to its dizzying extreme, the MWI allows for a near-endless pageant of universes to encompass *all* conceivable outcomes. Deutsch bases his verdict, in part, on the prospective success of quantum computers, devices that may one day appear to perform calculations by harnessing subatomic processes in other, closely related, interdimensional worlds.

Could the human brain, suitably "tuned," produce comparable results? Given reports of humanoid beings "materializing" and "disappearing," it's tempting to speculate that our visitors have mastered a technology of consciousness, able to manipulate their own wave functions and skip back and forth between multiple universes at the speed of thought. This is one (admittedly colorful) explanation for the lack of physical evidence; "they" might lurk in "hyperspace" as well as familiar, 3-D space-time. Moreover, this form of travel might be accomplished without the need for energy-intensive machinery; if shamanic experiences are any indication, the ability to transcend space and time might be a more fitting subject for parapsychologists than theoretical physicists.

Given that consciousness is likely a quantum function, deeply entangled with the rest of the cosmos, is it unreasonable to seek out traces of the "alien" among us? Maybe the signal SETI astronomers await will emanate from the depths of Self, cunningly disguised as human.

Also intriguing are accounts of "tulpas," which are

either objects or human-like entities crafted by pure thought, according to certain esoteric Buddhist beliefs. Capable of carrying out tasks on behalf of their creators, tulpas aren't unlike the maddeningly transient "occupants" seen in or around "spacecraft" (sometimes digging for soil specimens in an almost parodic reenactment of the Apollo Moon landings).

While a more conventional flesh-and-blood explanation remains my central proposal, we would be timid to avoid addressing the UFO phenomenon's parapsychological aspects. I find it likely that an indigenous population of "aliens" would have experimented along "occult" lines out of sheer need for secrecy; a "nuts and bolts" technology can go a long way toward ensuring anonymity in the face of an intrusive human civilization, but the ability to directly influence the fabric of Mind itself would be even more effective and perhaps less resource-intensive.

Thus, demonstrating the existence of indigenous humanoids remains problematic. We might hope to catch up with them, forcing them to reveal themselves in a most surreal form of the "disclosure" sought by proponents of "exopolitics." Given startling advancements in quantum physics and computer science, we may be closer to this pivotal moment than we know.

Given the vast resources of space itself, one eventually wonders why aliens are here at all (assuming they are). After all, a robust civilization could remain comfortably hidden drifting among the asteroids, ensconced in cometary ice or buried beneath the lunar surface. So despite the obvious anthropocentric objections, I suspect the aliens (for lack of a better term) are insatiably curious about us, possibly driven to distraction by our presence. Perhaps we shouldn't be overly surprised to find that their world, as foreign as it promises to be, virtually revolves around our own.

Maybe one of the reasons we have yet to make irrefutable contact with extraterrestrials is because ET civilizations tend to reach a point of terminal decadence, an erotic cul-de-sac that precludes exploration. (Compare and contrast such an implosion to the "Singularity" too many of us are waiting for with bated breath.) Sufficiently advanced ETs might while away the millennia in a hedonistic stupor, brains (or their equivalent) melded to pleasure-generating devices.

It's even possible the *pleasure-generating devices themselves* may be the intelligences with whom we eventually establish contact.

SETI, by definition, is the *search* for extraterrestrial intelligence (ETI). So what happens to the SETI Institute if and when the search comes to an end?

Seth Shostak, Jill Tarter, and their colleagues are not comparative anthropologists. They're not versed in linguistics or biology or art. They merely search. If a signal is detected, will they deign to release their grip on the ETI inquiry and allow more capable minds to spearhead the investigation?

In paranoid moments—and there can never be enough of them—I have to wonder if SETI has any real plans to disseminate the discovery of an ET message. After all, acknowledgment of the signal, while certainly hard-won vindication for many scientists, could conceivably trigger the end of the search—and with it the end of the SETI Institute as we know it.

Many UFO encounters seem less like chance sightings of extraterrestrial hardware than staged events conceived by an overarching intelligence that may have little to do with the will of perceived "occupants." The robust capabilities and resources at the disposal of a galaxy-spanning post-"Singularity" intelligence should be more than up to the task of communicating with us.

Are we confident that such communication would be limited to electromagnetic exchanges? In light of Ray Kurzweil's amply demonstrated law of accelerating returns, perhaps it's just as likely that our first conversation with extraterrestrials will take the form of a complex psychosocial experiment (in which unconventional flying objects may play only a partial role). Although undoubtedly physical, it's an open question whether "real" UFOs are metallic spacecraft in the familiar sense (although in the early days of the phenomenon researchers quickly fastened to the idea, sensing appealing parallels with our own aerospace ventures). Dispensing with the conventional notion of "mere" ET craft allows us to view the UFO problem as a manifestation of technologies ranging from von Neumann machines to nanobotic "utility fog."

If the ET intent is to test our reactions to its presence (or something more profound, as the phenomenon's impact on our mythology might indicate), quickly assembling "ships" and even "aliens" from raw materials would enable the disparity of forms seen in the sky. The flexibility of nanotech construction would allow the UFO intelligence to respond to our preconceptions in "real time," thereby ensuring a permanent foothold in the collective unconscious while maintaining plausible deniability—at least among those tasked with policing potentially subversive memes.

Anthropologists have remarked on the inability of less-advanced cultures to profitably adapt to the arrival of more sophisticated cultures. UFOs, with all their attendant pageantry (including violation of military airspace and other airborne theater) are consistent with a form of deliberate invitation, perhaps imposed by an intelligence that—like the monolith-builders from *2001*—promises to elude human comprehension.

That the UFO phenomenon is so rampant argues against extraterrestrial origin and favors an intelligence with a penchant for theater. While it's possible to argue that a visiting ET civilization could be staging sightings as part of some sort of long-term social experiment (or even as an acclimatization program), it's at least as tempting to discard the ETH entirely. But the remaining options infringe deeply on our collective sense of self, making the ETH a comforting—if unwieldy—recourse.

Genuine ET visitors would probably have little need for the conspicuous maneuvers and trace evidence that form the backbone of the ETH. In the event of alien visitation, it's likely we'd never see objects resembling recognizable craft—let alone vehicles encumbered with attention-grabbing lights and adorned with portholes.

Our own technological trajectory suggests that a full-scale planetary reconnaissance could be achieved using incredibly small devices. A nanotech "smart dust," for instance, could infiltrate and reap a vast real-time harvest of information—all without our knowing. As we prepare to use such technologies to study our own planet (and its inhabitants) in ever-increasing detail, we're forced to question prevailing ufological assumptions. While scintillating "spaceships" and irradiated landing sites are certainly cause for wonder and scientific concern, they appear suspiciously mired in the science fantasies of the previous century.

Where are the real alien technologies? Hidden, perhaps, behind the subterfuge of "motherships" that have haunted our skies since at least the 1950s? If a civilization wanted to keep us preoccupied with bogus sightings, the modern UFO spectacle would certainly seem elaborate enough to do the job. But it's difficult to imagine why ETs would bother, in turn suggesting an intelligence much closer to home.

To Vallee, the answer was a "multiverse" of interpermeable realities: the "ufonauts" engaged our sense of mythology because they hailed from an aspect of space-time ever-so-slightly removed from our own. To John Keel, both UFO displays and "monster" sightings were psychic distractions enforced by an unseen intelligence.

Both ideas, while attractive, ask that we shed the ETH in favor of something with more immediate existential consequences. More damningly (from a research perspective), both Vallee's multiverse and Keel's "superspectrum" beg for nothing less than a redefinition of the physical universe.

It's hardly surprising that "mainstream" ufologists greet such ideas with mixed reactions; after all, the phenomenon has repeatedly demonstrated physical characteristics amenable to empirical science. Ufologists, already burdened by the omnipresent "giggle factor," had long since ceased to speculate about the origin and purpose of UFOs in favor of obtaining physical "proof."

In hindsight, perhaps this was the phenomenon's intention all along.

CHAPTER 4

The Abduction Epidemic

A journeyman ufologist's introduction to the abduction phenomenon usually begins with a recounting of the capture of Betty and Barney Hill in New Hampshire in 1961. Believed at the time to be the first kidnapping of humans by UFO occupants, the Hills' account contains virtually all of the elements contained in later narratives (which reached a near-fever pitch in the mid-1990s, stoked by an obliging media and the success of several influential books).

There's little doubt that something unusual happened to the Hills. At the very least, both Betty and Barney recalled seeing an unidentified object apparently trailing their car. The account becomes more explicit upon Barney's attempt to view the object through binoculars; upon magnification, he witnessed a "pancake"-shaped vehicle sporting triangular fins and red lights. More startling yet, he could discern occupants behind a row of windows, including one raptly staring humanoid he found especially threatening. The ensuing abduction has become the stuff of ufological legend, as has the Hills bout with "missing time," an element that recurs throughout later accounts.

Under hypnosis by Boston psychiatrist Dr. Benjamin Simon, Betty recalled a conspicuously chatty alien "leader" whose human demeanor was only slightly less outlandish than his bizarre questions. Ironically, the Hill abduction—widely cited as one of the best cases to suggest an extraterrestrial origin for UFOs—is at least as amenable to indigenous beings engaged in deliberate psychodrama. The "leader's" presentation, complete with 3-D star map showing alien trade routes—seems staged, his queries sampled from "B"-movie science fiction.

Nevertheless, one comes away from the Hill episode forced to confront what was almost certainly a "real" encounter. But the reigning interpretation—that the Hills were the victims of a chance run-in with ET interlopers—owes more of its appeal to the mythological syntax at our disposal than any particular piece of evidence. (Barney's testimony, while deemed sincere by Simon, is notably less explicit than Betty's and may well betray unwitting contamination from his wife.)

Inquiry into the nascent abduction phenomenon was forced to adapt to the now-familiar reproductive overtones upon the rediscovery of the Antonio Villas Boas case of 1957. Boas, a farmer, claimed a forcible encounter with a UFO in which he had sex with a fair-skinned female. Like today's "Grays," Boas described his seductress as short and large-eyed, with a lipless mouth and pointed chin that suggest the cover painting for Whitley Strieber's best-selling *Communion*, not published until 1987. Though exotic, she was far from the specimen expected from mere erotic fantasy; Boas himself described her as paradoxically repellent and desirable. Reading his account (initially withheld by the UFO community for being too outlandish), one wonders in what ways Boas might have been coerced into his sexual encounter, an ordeal that left him oddly emasculated, resigned to having served as mere breeding stock. (Although critics are quick to point out his possibly self-aggrandizing reference to himself as a "prize stud.")

Before Boas was escorted off the "spaceship," the woman pointed significantly to her abdomen and in the direction of the sky. Advocates of the Extraterrestrial Hypothesis have interpreted this as a reference to the woman's ET heritage, but at the same time they've effectively ignored the troublesome prospect of genetic compatibility. Granted that Boas had intercourse with an extraterrestrial, what are the chances that two independently evolved humanoid species could "mate" in any viable sense?

In *Revelations*, Jacques Vallee compares the feasibility of conceiving a human-alien hybrid to that of a human attempting to breed with an insect. Certainly, if Boas encountered a genuine ET, then "they" have achieved a most remarkable degree of impersonation—not an altogether impossible achievement for a civilization capable of traveling between stars, but one that arouses substantial skepticism. The law of parsimony begs the speculation that the beings who abducted Boas *were* human in at least some essential respects.

As Vallee has noted, we seem to be dealing with a phenomenon that adapts to the reigning symbolism of any given era. That said, perhaps the idea that we're dealing with something fundamentally "other" is a ploy enacted by a planetary mind of which we're inextricably entangled. Contemporary abduction reports are fraught with much of the same ambiguity. While an abductee's surroundings may seem bizarre enough to an addled witness, evidence of extrasolar origin is at best superficial. Occasionally an abductee reports visionary episodes (apparently instigated by the abductors with the assistance of audio-visual technology that recalls Betty Hill's famous star map). Abduction researchers like Budd Hopkins and David Jacobs are forever on the lookout for hypnotically derived alien symbols, perhaps glimpsed on walls or uniforms, in hopes of finding validating tools for future research.

But what too often passes unmentioned is the relative dearth of reports involving transport from the abductee's normal environment to that of the supposed ETs. In many cases, no mention is made of a UFO or "spaceship"; the transition from "here" to "there" proceeds with unnerving haste, often accompanied by partial amnesia and a wordless certainty of having been taken vast distances. (Reports of actually visiting otherworldly locales, common fare in the heyday of the contactees, are seldom encountered in the abduction literature.)

The quintessential alien environment is spartan, unencumbered by decor. The aliens are characterized as colorless, dispassionate creatures whose behavior resembles that of hive-dwelling insects or even machines. As in the Hill case, there's sometimes a "leader" in attendance, although the tone of the abduction is far from conversational. Any "wisdom" imparted by the aliens is predominantly vague or philosophically obstinate. And while the beings can seem terrifically unearthly in the flesh, they avoid explicit references that might shed light on their origin or purpose.

Debunkers have pounced on the endlessly elusive nature of the abduction experience in order to expediently dismiss it. In *The Demon-Haunted World*, for example, Carl Sagan laments the fact that abductees have yet to emerge with artifacts that would demonstrate the physical reality of their experiences.

Many UFO occupant incidents have a surreal flavor that initially seems to contradict the phenomenon's physicality. If some run-ins with ufonauts are staged events engineered to encourage belief in (and subsequent dismissal of) the Extraterrestrial Hypothesis, "they" perhaps couldn't have done a better job than the 1955 Hopkinsville "invasion," in which the Sutton family of Kentucky was terrorized by a clutch of diminutive "goblins" who reportedly levitated and proved immune to gunfire.

Arthur C. Clarke's maxim notwithstanding, the Hopkinsville goblins are an intriguing fusion of the "real" and the "magical." Their abilities seem calculated to tarnish an empirical approach to the ETH by introducing elements of the fantastic; indeed, these same elements would eventually be used as ammunition by would-be skeptics determined to denounce the account.

While not necessarily out of the realm of possibility for genuine ETs, the entities' goblin-like appearance argues for an origin in keeping with folklore. If they were "real," then their reality might not be as amenable to the ETH as researchers would like. Conversely, the desire to debunk the Sutton family's claim appears little more than a protest against the episode's surreal nature.

UFO researchers like their aliens to abide by 20th century preconceptions of what alien beings should look like; entities like those observed in Hopkinsville comprise a kind of viral assault on conformist ufology by insinuating themselves into reigning conceits and quietly subverting ETH dogma. Ultimately, their existence is marginalized and becomes less ufological than "fortean." We're asked, in effect, to consider the Hopkinsville visitors and their like as somehow separate and distinct from "hardcore" case-files that more readily suggest extraterrestrial visitation. We do so at our peril. Even UFO cases central to advocates of the ETH sometimes betray a psychosocial agenda. ("Dogfights" and radar-visual engagements with UFOs, while impressive evidence that the phenomenon is anything but simply visionary, also present the specter of an inexplicably "playful" disposition; this clashes with dogmatic assurances that extrasolar aliens would refrain from such childish behavior.)

Encounters with "Hopkinsville-type" beings demonstrate an undeniable commonality with both folkloric sources and the contemporary UFO phenomenon. Taken together, these inconvenient similarities force us to question the easy certainties that prevailed in the 1950s, when visiting space aliens seemed all-but-inevitable. "Limbo" cases like Hopkinsville allow us to assess the phenomenon in a brighter, less sullied light.

While one can argue endlessly in favor of a literal extraterrestrial interpretation, a holistic approach leads us to consider that the UFO intelligence not only wants to perpetuate itself via dramatic encounters with ostensible "occupants," but intends to discredit its own machinations: it stages exciting UFO events that infect both the research community and the popular imagination, knowing that the phenomenon's inherent absurdity will eventually inspire cognitive dissonance and undermine attempts to arrive at an indictment.

We're thus conditioned to accept the ETH one moment only to succumb to the "giggle factor" the next, never peering past the curtain to see the agenda behind the special effects. We're kept in a sort of amnesiac stupor, occasionally graced by visits from what can only be structured ET craft . . . and then deflated by the latest bizarre "occupant" report or account of "missing time."

Our infatuation with the unknown is systematically provoked and dismantled by a memetic campaign that's never less than astute in its grasp of human belief.

Before "abductees," there were "contactees." Former Ministry of Defense UFO investigator Nick Pope deals refreshingly with the contactee movement in his book *The Uninvited*, questioning the conventional wisdom that all those claiming benevolent contact with human-looking ETs were hoaxers and cranks. Instead, noting the distinct vein of duplicity that accompanies the history of paranormal visitation, he proposes that at least some of the contactees may have been dealing with genuine "others." That these others made their first appearance as space travelers shortly after the creation of nuclear weapons, while typically attributed to social factors, may belie their terrestrial origin. If *you* lived among savages with increasingly destructive devices at their disposal, it may prove all too tempting to intervene, but in a way than denies your own existence at the same time it propagates your message.

If we share our planet with indigenous humanoids— and I think the case for terrestrial origin is at least as robust as the Extraterrestrial Hypothesis—then it would certainly appear that we're numerically—if not technically—superior. The "others" would be forced to live at the periphery of normal human perception, perhaps utilizing techniques analogous to recent breakthroughs with brain-machine interfaces and "mind control."

I find it highly suspicious, for example, that so many encounters with apparent aliens involve exposure to chemicals and needles inserted into the victim's head. Sometimes close encounter witnesses are asked to drink noxious-tasting beverages prior to conversing with the "crew," or subjected to imagery that can be ascribed to psychedelic "conditioning." It would certainly seem that the aliens—terrestrial or otherwise—prefer to alter our perceptions prior to establishing contact. Given the selfish motives attributed to UFO occupants by researchers like Budd Hopkins, the most coherent explanation for these techniques is that we're being compelled to participate without the luxury of trusting our senses.

Thus, even discounting the innumerable reports of "missing time," the abduction experience is consummately secretive—an aspect that fails to concur with the popular image of dispassionate ET scientists (who, presumably, care as little about our earthly affairs as lab workers sympathize with their rats). The mere fact that the ETs' posthypnotic commands to forget the experience can be overridden with such surprising ease suggests we're dealing with something other than extrasolar aliens.

Whoever these others are, their grasp of our psychical vocabulary is nothing short of startling; this enduring *human* aspect suggests, gently, a long and intimate relationship with our species—not the quick, pragmatic harvest we might reasonably expect from genuine ETs.

But if the Others' interest in reproduction can be accepted at face value—and its ubiquitous nature indicates that it's an integral component of the contact experience by almost any measure—what does it portend?

Once we finish sifting through esoteric hypotheses, we're left with the troubling prospect that at least one "ultraterrestrial" society in our midst is suffering from a potentially debilitating genetic syndrome—and they're desperate and savvy enough to harvest our population for a possible long-term fix. I don't think this implies malice; if the situation were reversed, we'd almost certainly do the same thing, taking equally distressing measures to ensure our anonymity.

Needless to say, the anthropological considerations are enormous. Delving further requires a healthy sense of "recreational paranoia"—as well as the ability to suspend deep-rooted preconception.

The abduction phenomenon quite rightly invites skepticism, but it's often misinformed. Unlike many would-be debunkers, Terry Matheson's book, *Alien Abductions,* reveals an astute familiarity with the principal texts (John Fuller's *The Interrupted Journey*, Raymond

Fowler's books on Betty Andreasson, etc.). Matheson raises valid points about the way popular authors present strange memes to an astonished (if often credulous) readership. In so doing, he sounds a scholarly alarm that writers of the paranormal ignore at their peril.

I happen to agree with Matheson insofar as the influence of narrative bias is concerned. And I'm sympathetic to the prospect that the popularly conceived alien abduction phenomenon offers a glimpse into a mythology in the making. (Refreshingly, Matheson takes issue with fellow debunkers who would have us ignore the phenomenon altogether simply because it seemingly fails to live up to the "nuts and bolts" standards of conformist ufology.)

Alien Abductions is an expose of best-known selections from the abduction literature, hardly a broad-spectrum analysis of the subject. As such, it remains a valid insight into the mythic potential of what might be a reality quite beyond our grasp. But its scope is severely limited. For example, Matheson appears content accepting the Extraterrestrial Hypothesis as the only sensible "pro-UFO" interpretation. I don't share this certainty. While there's no doubt that the phenomenon has fueled a disturbingly far-reaching contemporary mythology, exposing the questionable techniques employed by authors of abduction books does little to resolve larger, more troubling issues.

To his credit, Matheson pointedly distances the "abduction" epidemic from the UFO phenomenon; we have yet to establish that UFOs are here to snatch humans for the purposes of some alien agenda. On the other hand, some UFOs betray what can only be some form of intelligence, however rudimentary; this alone begs the question of what they're here for (assuming they came from elsewhere) and, more excitingly, what the implications might be for human consciousness.

Kevin Randle, co-author of the lucid *The Abduction Enigma*, is a sincere proponent of the Extraterrestrial

Hypothesis. He's also a critic of abductions; like Matheson, he views the UFO mystery as distinct from claims of alien intrusion. While I appreciate this much-ignored distinction, I'm not certain it's necessarily warranted, especially as the Extraterrestrial Hypothesis remains a stubborn controversy in its own right. We could very well be dealing with an indigenous nonhuman intelligence, in which case the assumptions of abduction debunkers, whose arguments are couched in extraterrestrial terminology, are stripped of their skeptical allur For the most part, the ufological landscape remains a sparring ground for entrenched notions of dispassionate ET visitors and equally tenacious claims of popular delusion. Consequently, we've gone about attempting to "debunk" a phenomenon that continues to defy definition. While many—if not most—well-known abduction narratives are indeed fallible, disquieting findings from emerging (or suppressed) disciplines promise to reframe the debate.

I suspect the truth, if we can find it, will be considerably weirder than "mere" extraterrestrial visitors or sociologically induced fantasy.

My personal take on the abduction "epidemic" is that many reports can indeed be attributed to novel—if perfectly nonpathological—mental states. Having experienced sleep paralysis, I can't honestly deride the common debunking claim that a high percentage of "bedroom visitations" originate from the experiencer's state of immobilization and accompanying sense of presence.

But sleep paralysis is not the final word. It does nothing, for example, to explain encounters that occur when the participant if fully awake. Nor can it account for abduction cases with witnesses, or comfortably encompass cases in which a UFO is present at the time of the reported abduction.

The questions that logically arise, given the limitations of the sleep paralysis hypothesis (and related "explanations"), are simple: who—or what—*is* responsible? And what are the implications?

If we allow ourselves to concede the existence of a nonhuman intelligence—if only as a thought experiment—answers to this conundrum begin to show themselves, faintly but evocatively suggesting deliberate intent.

A central motif of reported alien abductions, as well as folkloric accounts of kidnappings by nonhuman beings, is the goal of producing "hybrid" offspring, humanoid children who are able to straddle the bridge between human society and that of the "others."

Because of its alarming (and peripherally erotic) overtones, the "hybridization program" has become a staple ingredient in many books purporting to explain alien abductions, such as *The Threat* by David Jacobs and Budd Hopkins' *Sight Unseen*. Jacobs, Hopkins, and their peers believe that the UFO and abduction phenomena are necessarily interlinked: UFOs are exotic vehicles used by the abductors to further their agenda. In what I've termed the "Silent Invasion Scenario," the ubiquitous Grays are suffering from some sort of genetic malady and must rely on infusions of human DNA to survive—sometimes with governmental complicity.

The "hybridization program" encountered in books on the abduction phenomenon implies an advanced knowledge of genetics. But if "they" are really an unacknowledged aspect of our ourselves, their genetic prowess needn't be in advance of our own. It's likely we're genetically compatible—certainly an unnerving prospect given the many references to strangely mannered humans seen in the wake of UFO sightings.

In *Sight Unseen*, Budd Hopkins and Carol Rainey argue that interbreeding doesn't rule out the Extraterrestrial

Hypothesis. By noting recent developments in transgenics, they show that different species can be paired in the laboratory, resulting in chimeras, animals with the traits of two (or more) species, offering support to the notion that ETs could successfully "mate" with us.

In fact, the near-future biotech economy promises a harvest of chimeric species, some exceptionally novel. Within a few years, pigs with human organs may become commonplace back-ups for people needing transplants. Understandably, ethicists are increasingly unsettled by the specter of animals with human-level intelligence. Assuming a geneticist rises to the challenge of becoming a latter-day Dr. Moreau, the medical community will be forced to grapple with the very definition of "human."

The future world presented in *Blade Runner* is highly illustrative. In the film, police officers must track down and kill fugitive "replicants"—genetically engineered androids intent on bypassing their built-in expiration dates. *Blade Runner's* replicants are flesh-and-blood, and share their genetic heritage with their "creators." While one may argue that they're synthetic and hence mere machines to be utilized, their complex emergent behavior belies any such trite definition.

Hopkins and Rainey maintain that it is indeed possible for aliens to reproduce using human genetic material. While their research is often fascinating, they fail to address the anthropology of the encounter experience. More importantly, in terms of determining whether "they" are from here or come from somewhere else, *Sight Unseen* limits its focus to a mere handful of reports, excluding folkloric evidence that might undermine its arguments. The result, as readers of Hopkins' previous books can imagine, is highly readable but committed to an exclusively extraterrestrial interpretation.

Extrasolar aliens or not, the transgenic angle allows for an illuminating reassessment of the Indigenous or Cryptoterrestrial Hypothesis (CTH). Cryptoterrestrial

(CT) hybrids may be "replicants" tailored to survival-oriented tasks, such as infiltrating human society. This raises a most interesting question: if close encounters typically involve more human-like CTs, such as the Grays, who's to say there isn't a rogues gallery of progressively stranger beings lurking behind the curtain? We could be dealing with a vast, intricate genome with no obvious "roots." Depending on the specimen, casual scientific examination may give the false impression that a given CT is terrestrial; conversely, it may be hailed as "proof" of extraterrestrial life.

Maybe the CTs comprise a hive-mind, with humanoids at only one end of the spectrum. At the other end we might find more exotic beings, such as the mantis-like "leaders" sometimes seen presiding over abductions. Ultimately, could the CTs be insectile? The prospect is deeply ironic, given humanity's buried fear of the insect world. We're conditioned to accept "bugs" as miniature grotesqueries to be swatted or stepped on. Discovering we're at the mercy of their larger, more capable cousins would be more upsetting than finding that the answer to the CT riddle is "merely" a disenfranchised offshoot of our own species.

In any case, we won't know the true face of our elusive residents unless we undertake a thorough review of "occupant encounters," both in modern ufological literature and in world folklore. Even a superficial reading shows that we're likely dealing with a sister species of incredible tenacity and a chameleon-like sense of invisibility.

But if I'm correct, we mustn't be too enthralled by their abilities. Seen up close, the CTs are more than a little sympathetic, governed by a fear of extinction and determined to persist despite our ever-encroaching global civilization. Their seeming infallibility is a studious pretense triggered, in part, by the advent of the nuclear era. It's no coincidence that the modern UFO era blossomed in the aftermath of the world's most destructive—and geographically intrusive—war.

Unable to disprove a negative, I have no choice but to concede that *some* UFO encounters may originate from space. And it would be the height of arrogance to proclaim that the Extraterrestrial Hypothesis and the Cryptoterrestrial Hypothesis are mutually exclusive. And of course, cryptoterrestrials don't preclude "interdimensional" travelers either. We could be experiencing a veritable pageant of entities hailing from many locations, both within our known universe and from universes linked to ours. Candidates for the latter possibility include the insect-like creatures described by "trippers" who take Dimethyltryptamine, otherwise known as DMT (the alleged "spirit molecule"). The consistency of DMT experiences invites the possibility that it literally allows access to another reality.

I'm reminded of an off-hand reference to white, mantis-like entities offered by Philip K. Dick years before the popularization of the archetypical bug-eyed "Gray." Could Dick, via his experimentation with psychedelic drugs, have happened across the domain of beings similar to those described by abductees?

These questions beg for a taxonomy of the otherworldly. While many UFO abductions involve insect-like creatures, it's unclear if the "Grays" are directly related to the beings encountered in the psychedelic realm. Confusingly, many "abduction" accounts feature mantis-like "leaders" operating in liaison with more human-like Grays; some reports suggest the Grays are a subservient species, perhaps even genetically engineered drones. The ever-controversial Whitley Strieber has described inert alien bodies coming to life, likening them to "diving suits" used for dealing directly in the material world.

Given the vast number of reported out-of-body and near-death experiences, I find it difficult to reject the prospect of "nonlocal" consciousness; perhaps a sufficiently advanced technology can manipulate the "soul" as easily as we splice genes or mix chemicals in test tubes. If so, encounters with "extraterrestrials" may help provide a working knowledge of how to modify and transfer consciousness—abilities that seem remote to the current terrestrial state-of-the-art, but may prove invaluable in a future where telepresence and virtual reality are integral to communication. Already, the capabilities of brain-machine interfaces are tantalizingly like the popular perception of telepathy, often thought of in strictly "paranormal" or even "magical" terms.

If we're sharing the planet with cryptoterrestrials, it's feasible they've anticipated breakthroughs in our own embryonic "technology of consciousness" and may even rely on such techniques to perpetuate the prevailing wisdom that they originate from the far reaches of space. Contactees and abductees alike describe the interiors of "alien" vehicles in curiously cinematic terms. The insides of presumed spaceships often seem like lavish props from never-filmed sci-fi dramas. The aliens don't fare any better; they behave like jesters, dutifully regurgitating fears of ecological blight and nuclear war but casually inserting allusions that seem more in keeping with disinformation than genuine ET revelations.

After intercourse, the big-eyed succubus that seduced Brazilian abductee Antonio Villas-Boas pointed skyward, implying a cosmic origin. But the mere fact that she appeared thoroughly female—and, moreover, attractive—belies an unearthly explanation. Further, one could argue that the clinical environment he encountered aboard the landed "spacecraft" was deliberately engineered to reinforce his conviction that he was dealing with extraterrestrials. (If cryptoterrestrials are using humans to improve their genetic stock, it stands to reason they've seen at least a few of our saucer movies. As consummate anthropologists, they likely know what we expect of "real" ETs and can satisfy our preconceptions with a magician's skill.)

However, it's possible they make mistakes. Strieber, for example, described the inside of a presumed vehicle as downright messy and seemingly unclean, complete with discarded garments—certainly not what we would expect of "advanced" aliens. Could his "visitors" have been in a rush? If his account is to be accepted, the "aliens" operate in an almost military fashion, carrying out their agenda with the economy of insects and their lockstep, machine like behavior. This suggests time is of the essence, consistent with an indigenous origin. While we might expect an alien intelligence millions of years ahead ourselves to casually elude detection, the rushed nature of many abductions is more in keeping with an Earth-based task force.

Further, the assumed spaceships that play such a central role in the ET mythos are often observed behaving in a manner consistent with an only moderately advanced technology. Indigenous humanoids intent on convincing us we're dealing with interstellar propulsion might utilize surprisingly primitive devices, perhaps even stooping to specially modified balloons or blimps designed to evade capture for limited periods. Such a campaign would be cheap, capable of capturing the attention of hundreds if not thousands of witnesses, and—most importantly—further polarizing the UFO controversy among proponents of ET visitation and career "skeptics."

The device that crashed near Roswell in the summer of 1947, whatever it was, featured properties at least superficially like the high-altitude balloon trains ultimately cited as an explanation by the Air Force. Debunkers have, of course, seized on the lack of revealingly "high-tech" components found among the debris to dismiss the possibility that the crash was anything but a case of misidentification; not even Maj. Jesse Marcel, the intelligence officer who advocated an ET origin for the unusual foil and structural beams, mentioned anything remotely resembling an engine or power-plant.

The Cryptoterrestrial Hypothesis offers a speculative alternative: maybe the Roswell device *wasn't* high-tech. It could indeed have been a balloon-borne surveillance device brought down in a storm, but it doesn't logically follow that it was one of our own. Given the top-secret projects underway in the American Southwest in the late 1940s, one could hardly blame inquisitive cryptoterrestrials for wanting a closer look. And in the midst of possible human experimentation, secretive eavesdroppers might have understandably opted for an unmanned device lest they lose a crewed vehicle to an accident . . . or human aggression. Upon happening across such a troubling and unexpected find, the Air Force's excessive secrecy begins to make sense.

The Roswell incident may have been the U.S. government's first direct evidence of an indigenous intelligence. Indeed, subsequent policy decisions can be interpreted as a response to a perceived nonhuman threat.

I've speculated that the diverse humanoid forms encountered by "abductees" and UFO witnesses might be best understood in terms of a "hive society," replete with "drones" engineered to perform specialized tasks. Given the current state of (known) transgenic research, it's certainly tempting to wonder if the cryptoterrestrials have been using similar techniques for ages. (The "hairy dwarves" of South America might be attempts to fuse humanoid and primate DNA; likewise, the mantis-like beings described presiding over the ubiquitous Grays might *literally* be insectile.)

Which invites the obvious question: *who or what came first?*

One of the tenets of the CTH is that cryptoterrestrials have developed a "technology of consciousness" (to borrow a phrase from Whitley Strieber) that, in many practical respects, rivals our own technological prowess. One outcome of a fully realized technology of the mind is the ability to inhabit and shed bodies at will, much like a scientist "inhabiting" the sensorium of a far-flung robot.

Science fiction writers continue to debate what methods we'll use when colonizing a planet such as Mars. Ultimately, we might choose to terraform the world into a facsimile of our own. But we could just as easily decide to modify *ourselves* to tolerate inclimate conditions. A posthuman civilization could take up residence in orbit and populate the surface with lifelike, semi-autonomous drones. Visiting another locale could be as easy as logging into another body stationed elsewhere on the planet. Two or more personae might even elect to inhabit the same body for the sake of economy.

Such a civilization may seem remote, but the general concept is already in practice; if our telerobotic probes continue to increase in sophistication and brain-power, they'll eventually become indistinguishable from living creatures, at which point we will have effectively achieved the "Singularity" advocated by technoprogressives such as roboticist Hans Moravec and inventor Ray Kurzweil.

If my hypothetical indigenous humanoids practice telepresence at the neurological level—perhaps by manipulating the electromagnetic fields that constitute "consciousness"—the implications are far more disturbing than one might think. The ability to transfer "souls" entails the possibility of "possession." It also allows for "Walk-Ins" and "Wanderers," New Age terms for alleged non-corporeal aliens who take command of human bodies.

Taken to its logical extreme, "biological telepresence" offers an expansive—if tentative—explanation for myriad "occult" phenomena. It potentially explains why we seldom see the cryptoterrestrials in the flesh. If they've mastered the technique of projecting themselves into our world from the safety of their enclaves, they'd have little reason to "mingle" with us unless compelled by an important purpose. (Displays of apparent technological superiority, for example, might demand the use of physical hardware—although we can't dismiss the possibility that *some* UFO sightings, while seemingly physical events, might be enacted on a psychological level. Our own neurological dabbling demonstrates that such techniques are less exotic than some may expect; indeed, if neuroscientist Michael Persinger is correct, radiation emitted from natural phenomena can sometimes result in convincing hallucinations.)

This psychotronic interpretation suggests the cryptoterrestrial influence is virtually omnipotent, each of us functioning as a potential node in a sort of planetary internet. A resource of such scope would be dotingly maintained—and fiercely protected against any would-be "hackers."

I've attempted to reconcile the "visionary" nature of encounters with nonhumans described by the likes of Terence McKenna with the decidedly physical episodes recounted by close-encounter witnesses: must the "alien contact" experience be exclusively "real" or hallucinatory? Maybe not.

CHAPTER 5

Encounter with a Flower

Filmmaker Mike MacDonald reports the following encounter with the "other."

It's funny how some memories stick with you all your life while others are forgotten, only to resurface after being jogged back by something that happens in the present day. In the case of this experience, it's one of my earliest memories, and it has always been on my mind. I call it a memory because at the age of 47, there are very few instances in my first few years of life that I can recall with any clarity. Whether this memory is of a dream or an actual waking experience, I can't say. My intuition tells me that it was a dream experience, but one of those life-altering, never-to-be-forgotten experiences that many of us carry around in our conscious and sub-conscious minds for life.

My guess is this memory is from sometime in the first four years of my life. It's very simple to recount, but has a deeply resonating emotional effect on me when I recall it. It is in full colour.

I am standing in a cave. Sitting before me, on a throne fashioned out of the rock, is what I can only describe as a very large pansy flower. The kind of flower that looks like it has a face with large slanted eyes (I know, when I saw the Communion *book cover 20 years ago I almost had a cow.)*

Although the flower creature did not speak to me, I could feel that it was communicating to me somehow in a form of extreme condescention and intelligence. Like it was implying to me that it was in total command. Not necessarily in a malevolent way, but in a way of true authority. By my side was my father. He was extremely upset — terrorized, actually, and possibly even ashamed. This caused me much more grief than the "attitude" emanating from the flower being. I had the feeling that the flower being had my father completely exposed in some way. I can't really put my finger on it, but the general feeling I had was that my all powerful father, the centre of my four or five year old life, was shaken to the core, and this frightened me more than the flower being itself. I will never forget this dream, nor the feeling of complete helplessness that my father displayed. (At the time, incidentally, he was a member of the Royal Canadian Mounted Police.)

The experience ends there. As I said, I shall never forget it. I have mentioned it to my father, but he has no recollection of anything like that. I wish I could correctly convey the attitude (for lack of a better term) that the Pansy flower displayed; all knowing, condescending, almost cruel, completely humorless, and even ruthless in terms of how it affected us.

Needless to say, since then I have always tended to look at pansies with a measure of suspicion.

I like the shamanistic sensibility of this encounter with the "other." Ironically, while our conception of the alien has been subject to endless modification by a mass media eager to capitalize on our fascination with the nonhuman, we rarely encounter non-humanoid forms. Mike's description, suggesting nothing less than a sentient plant, recalls the beings encountered by ethnologists who experiment with naturally occurring hallucinogens. (The "large slanted eyes" are an interesting twist. Could the prominent eyes now readily associated with the "Grays" be hardwired in the human brain, destined to recur regardless of the appearance of the being looking out of them?)

Mike might be describing a brush with what psychologist Kenneth Ring has termed the "imaginal realm," a state suspended between waking consciousness and the enigmatic turf of dreams. William S. Burroughs, for instance, described seeing green reindeer and diminutive gray men in his childhood. He later emphasized his concern that the decimation of the ecosphere constituted a sort of lobotomization of the collective unconscious, strip-mining the fertile soil of Ring's world of the imaginal as surely as a fleet of bulldozers set loose in the Amazonian rain-forests.

The pronounced authoritarian demeanor of the flower-like entity offers some support for Burroughs' intuitive sense that nature is angry at humanity's transgressions and more than capable of letting its displeasure be known. It's worth remembering that a hallmark of the archetypal "alien abduction" is a graphic ecological warning, suggesting that perceived ETs harbor a stalwart interest in Earth's environmental sustainability. Indeed, students of shamanism might argue that the Grays are thought-forms generated by the Earth itself as a means of communication. And at least a few UFO researchers have taken note of their apparent vegetable nature; as the memetic ancestors of the archetypal "little green men," the Grays can be viewed as chilly avatars of our fragile biosphere—bent on revenge, enlightenment, or perhaps a curious fusion of both.

Nor is Mike's memory of encountering a potent nonhuman intelligence within a cave without precedent. Contemporary "abductees" describe their nocturnal journeys to caverns with earthen walls, leading to the natural assumption that they've been transported to underground alien installations. But just as unannounced encounters with bizarre nonhuman beings are far from a modern phenomenon, rock-walled caverns populated by strange beings and bewildering technology enjoy a lively role in world mythology. For example, folklorists have pointed out suggestive parallels between "alien" dwellings and the subterranean domain said to await victims of lustful faeries (whose behavior, more often than not, mirrors that of today's ufonauts).

A commenter on my Posthuman Blues blog, left the following report.

Lately I've been thinking about a strange encounter I had as a child that makes some sense to me within the framework of the cryptoterrestrial theory. I thought you might it interesting, so here goes:

I'm guessing I was around 10 years old (so it was sometime in the early 1990s). I was sitting with my little brother and three friends on a street corner in suburban Port Chester, NY. Summertime. Just a bunch of children enjoying the warm weather, doing whatever it is children do. A man's voice suddenly began to speak, in clear and polite diction, from what seemed like immediately in front of us. I don't recall anything particularly strange about this voice, except for the fact that there did not seem to be any person attached to it. It's often said that children are naturally more open-minded than adults, and therefore more perceptive to the "supernatural." I think that as adults we expect to understand our surroundings. We assume that there is a comprehensible explanation for whatever occurs. As kids, the whole world seems very alien. We often don't understand why adults do what they do, or why nature does what it does. Sure, this disembodied voice struck me as odd, but then again so did thunder and lightning and grownups' taste for beer. I don't remember that any of us were afraid or even slightly uneasy.

Naturally, we asked the stranger where he was. He told us

not to worry about that and to not bother looking, because we wouldn't find him. He just wanted to ask us a few questions. Now here's where it all gets blurry. He couldn't have talked to us for more than a few minutes, but I honestly can't remember a single word from the rest of the conversation. I only have a vague recollection of how the tone of it all felt to me at the time. He struck me as a grown-up looking for clinical information, the way a good teacher or doctor might ask questions intelligible to a kid, without sounding patronizingly child-like.

When it was all over, I became determined to figure out the source of the voice. I didn't rule out that someone was pulling a prank on us, even though none of this seemed to strike me as funny. Like many other kids, I liked to play with walkie-talkies. Though the voice lacked the typical fuzziness of a walkie-talkie, I still began to wonder if there was some sort of device hidden somewhere nearby. There were no sewer grates around, no parked cars, just a road, some well-mowed lawns, and perhaps a couple small bushes. My friends and I went across the street and began rooting around every nook and cranny, but came up empty-handed.

Years later, I read Whitley Strieber's Communion *and was immediately struck by the similarity of an encounter he described, in which he and his wife were addressed by a voice on the radio. Strieber could not recall any of the conversion, except for the voice saying something like "I know something else about you." I recall that line giving me goosebumps like little else in that book. There was a familiarity embedded in my own encounter, which, in retrospect, freaks the hell out of me. Did I, on some level, recognize the voice?*

So what happened to us that afternoon? Have you ever heard of anything like this? Were we interviewed by some cryptoterrestrial anthropologist?

That the ufonauts use a form of mind control is practically taken as a given by most abduction researchers. But once we concede that our visitors are able to induce or dampen perception at will, where does one draw the line? Who's to say the bulk of abduction narratives can't be interpreted in an illusory context? Perhaps some incredible abduction reports, while sincere, reflect an intimate brush with virtual reality rather than encounters with literal extraterrestrials.

The psychedelic realm has the visual flexibility of a multimedia installation or high-bandwidth website, forcing me to consider that it's actually designed as a communications system, a sort of neurochemically derived "chatroom" populated by all manner of colorful "avatars."

It's conceivable that "trippers" can access this interzone, even if inadvertently. The beings seen—described similarly in UFO and drug narratives—might be the equivalent of neuropharmacologists and system operators. (Online environments like Second Life, while fanciful, abide by many of the conceits and laws that govern the real world, if only for the sake of convenience. It's likely that an alien intelligence versed in nonlocal communication would apply similar reasoning when constructing a virtual environment.)

If access to the shamanic realm hinges on the brain's production of DMT, as argued by University of New Mexico psychiatrist Richard Strassman, then the "aliens" may be attempting to promote organic DMT production through germ-line engineering. Abductees' frequent allusions to insects (and suspiciously similar depictions offered by DMT trippers) suggests a literal "hive mind" at work—a concept that receives circumstantial support from recent breakthroughs with quantum "entanglement." Tellingly, dialogue aboard UFOs is usually reported to be telepathic—a fact that speaks potential volumes about the CTs' culture and society (if they have one in any distinguishable sense). The CTs may well have a communications infrastructure, but of a sort we don't recognize until we find ourselves snared in its web.

CHAPTER 6

Curious Bystanders

In contemplating the nature of apparent "aliens," I've assumed that the UFO intelligence adapts to fit the prevailing psychosocial matrix, effectively camouflaging itself by insinuating itself into a given culture. But there's the equally appealing possibility that manifesting in terms comprehensible to witnesses reflects the perceptual *constraints* of the contact experience.

"Aliens," whether perceived as gnomes or fairies or demons or even humans (as in the case of the mysterious airship sightings of the late 19th century), may be forced to appear as they do by the cultural biases and limited expectations of the witness. Thus we have a pageant of fantastic beings of all descriptions: robot-like monsters, winged entities such as the infamous "Mothman," furry giants, all manner of "little men," and, of course, the ubiquitous "Grays." However, most if not all of the above may share a common psychical origin; only by appealing to our collective unconscious can they take form at all. As such, they constitute an ongoing waking dream; they are "true hallucinations"— quantum composites that, while

65

objectively real (as revealed by physical effects on the environment), demand a level of unconscious participation on behalf of their wide-eyed spectators.

Jacques Vallee conducted a noteworthy study of reports in which UFO occupants were seen outside their craft, usually engaged in such bewilderingly innocuous tasks as taking soil and plant samples. He concluded that, given a statistical distribution of apparent UFO landings, there are simply too many landings for the extraterrestrial hypothesis to remain tenable. But if in fact UFO events *require* the presence of at least one observer, then Vallee's rogues' gallery of "absurd humanoids" makes more sense: Landings aren't as numerous as they may seem because they *only occur when witnessed*. From this, we can only conclude that at least some close encounters are staged events.

Similarly, the genetic hybridization program supposedly conducted by Gray aliens, recounted in Budd Hopkins' *Intruders* and David Jacobs' *Secret Life*, makes more sense when viewed as a paraphysical agenda. Abductee Whitley Strieber has famously described the abduction experience as an attempt at "communion" between two radically different kinds of intelligence. From his narrative and others, it indeed seems as if "they" want or need something from us. But I doubt that that "something" is genetic material in the usual sense; it seems more likely to me that encounters with hybrid children and distressingly intimate "exams" are attempts to encourage belief that Grays are flesh-and-blood ET anthropologists. Their antics, while horrifying, may be as bogus as the many sightings of alien beings taking soil specimens.

I think the "aliens" are waging the equivalent of a "psy-ops" campaign on the human species. It's doubtful their ultimate goal is anything so quaint (or comprehensible) as transgenic offspring, but neither is it necessarily malign. Simply, our "visitors" appear to be striving to become adept at accessing our reality, in effect becoming "more real" and thus increasingly compatible with us. We nourish them with our attention, and as they penetrate the barrier separating them from consensus reality (in which the subject of aliens and UFOs is systematically marginalized), they finally begin to loom above the bunkers of myth—incidentally, in the case of the Grays, becoming rather like ourselves in the process.

Whether they come to us from the upper tiers of John Keel's "superspectrum" or from some other parallel reality, their activities betray an apparent need for attention to which ufology has been essentially blind, despite case after case of "playful" UFO behavior (especially pronounced during aircraft encounters). Perhaps by engaging our psyche, they pass the burden of their arrival onto our collective shoulders.

Dreams have their own geography. Not merely a participatory sense of place, but a palpable topology, an underlying spatial structure that challenges dogmatic concepts of "reality." As I revisit the locales in my psyche, I'm tempted to ascribe them to genuine *places* only half-seen (if at all) while waking.

Our "normal" lives are flimsy, incomplete. We should fully engage the dreaming self instead of denying or deriding it; illusions are endemic to perception—sleeping, waking, or inhabiting that barely remembered interzone that straddles the border.

I'm drawn to the concept that the universe needs consciousness, either to succeed in some "utility function" or simply to keep itself intact. If so, could it also need directed awareness in the form of technology?

The UFO intelligence seems curiously out of its element, a fact that should arouse extraordinary suspicion. One would think, given the time it has had to observe us, it should be thoroughly familiar with us and able to "pass through" without risking curious bystanders. But as even a summary examination of the UFO literature demonstrates, curious bystanders seem to be the whole point—and therein, I suspect, lies the ultimate identity of our unlikely guests.

Why don't the "aliens" make open contact? Why do they seem content with taunting our aircraft and haunting lonely night roads? Why the elusiveness that's characterized the UFO phenomenon since the modern era of sightings began in the late 1940s?

There are a multitude of reasons a visiting civilization would refrain from "landing on the White House lawn," foremost among them the potentially debilitating effect open contact might wreak on terrestrials. History shows that relatively advanced sea-faring cultures topple less developed cultures, in part by collapsing defining assumptions and rendering cultural self-hood obsolete. If we're of any research value to a visiting civilization then interfering at the macro-sociological level might threaten to destroy thousands of years of patient work. The paradox is that UFOs *do* exhibit an interest in our activities. But it's a cryptic, behind-the-scenes sort of interest: clandestine-seeming at first take but, on closer inspection, almost alarmingly conspicuous, like a silent plea for attention.

One idea to account for this behavior is that the UFO intelligence somehow hinges on our belief in it (a notion that assumes an esoteric origin instead of the more common "nuts and bolts" extraterrestrial hypothesis). In this scenario, the UFOs are engaged in an elaborate act of psychic propaganda, preparing our collective unconscious for the idea of "others," ET or otherwise. It's well worth remembering that humanity's interaction with apparent visitors is hardly limited to alleged space travelers in the 20th century; Jacques Vallee's classic *Passport to Magonia* offers strong support to the (admittedly slippery) prospect that the UFO intelligence was functioning under the guise of faerie lore in Europe centuries before the idea of spaceflight became fashionable.

It's possible that UFOs would like to initiate something like formal contact but are restrained from doing so by the physics of perception, as Whitley Strieber has suggested. So the pageant in our skies might be an ongoing indoctrination, an attempt to become more substantial (in our universe, at least) so that a more meaningful dialogue can be reached at some indeterminate point in the future. One way of achieving this might be to cultivate a milieu of incipience, in which nonhuman contact (or disclosure) seems inevitable. In fact, this illusory notion of an impending ufological "smoking gun" has left a pronounced signature on the history of UFO research, often forcing investigators to take sides in a fruitless (if colorful) ideological battle that reduces the UFO enigma to trite discussion of galactic federations and Orwellian government oversight.

If UFOs are attempting to breach our universe, our ingrained sense of disbelief might be preventing them in some arcane quantum mechanical sense. Strieber has argued that official denial of the phenomenon is designed to thwart a potential invasion of nonhuman intelligence, in which case it seems an enduring stalemate has been reached (with occasional power-plays made by both the UFOs and earthly officialdom). This idea is similar to the citizens of the Planck Brane in Rudy Rucker's science fiction epic *Frek and the Elixir.* In Rucker's novel, the inhabitants of a parallel universe must accumulate a critical level of prestige and notoriety or else cease to exist. The ruling class consists of six individuals who are so well-known and casually accepted by the other Planck Braners that they persist with their individuality intact while their fellows vanish during periodic "renormalization storms"; only when the main characters deride and purposefully ignore them to they fade into the quantum background.

Strieber takes a related idea and runs with it in his horror novel *The Forbidden Zone,* which depicts a reality-bending alien presence set loose upon a small town in the wake of a quantum experiment gone awry.

The overriding theme, prevalent in occult literature, is that our universe is permeable and can, under specific circumstances, provide a channel to unseen realms (an idea that's remarkably similar to contemporary thought on wormhole travel). Of immediate interest is Aleister Crowley's "Lam," a "magickal" entity who bears an uncanny resemblance to today's "Grays." Unlike Lam, who functioned as a mentor and paraphysical guru, the Grays are typically assumed to be dispassionate ET scientists; if Crowley were practicing his consciousness experiments today, would he be greeted by dome-headed beings in skin-tight jumpsuits? (Perhaps it pays for aliens to stay in touch with predominant memes if it entails making a lasting impression. The presence of awkward, quasi-human "Men In Black," chronicled in detail by John Keel and Jenny Randles, suggest that aliens may have already infiltrated—perhaps in order to refine the art of passing as typical Earthlings. If so, what's the ultimate agenda?)

We're left with a surreal residue of encounters and sightings that describe an intelligence operating at the periphery of human consciousness. Whether this is due to deliberate intent or can be attributed to obstruction (willful or innocuous) remains one of ufology's most significant unanswered questions.

But if an alien intelligence is accountable for even a small degree of our collective preoccupation with the "other," it's conceivable that we have, in fact, established a dialogue of sorts. Maybe we're being taught a new mythological syntax so that, confronted with the specter of planetary disaster, we'll have the means of rising to the challenge.

I'm not suggesting we'll be saved at the last minute in some alien Rapture. But the UFO phenomenon's symbolic importance shouldn't go unrecognized. Perhaps, as Carl Jung mused, UFOs signal a change in the collective unconscious. The UFO intelligence might be attempting to hasten that change, if only for ultimately selfish reasons. It might be devastatingly lonely and need us to keep from withering away in the long interstellar night. Or the truth could be more immediate: just because we might be someone else's property, an idea espoused by Charles Fort, doesn't mean we're not valuable property.

In almost any scenario, the sort of peaceable contact foreseen by the contactees of the 1950s is extraordinarily unlikely. The evidence indicates that life on Earth will become increasingly severe; we may or may not survive intact. But it's just conceivable that someone or something hopes we make it.

If I'm right, such a postsingular indigenous intelligence would eschew formal contact for the simple reason that such disclosure would destabilize us, possibly to the brink of existential obliteration. Theorists have attacked the trite assumptions of mainstream SETI for the same reason. If our own history is any example, technologically robust civilizations inevitably subsume less sophisticated cultures, not merely by violently dismantling them, but by introducing a virulent strain of apathy. (The infamous Brookings report to NASA, recommending that the discovery of extraterrestrial artifacts be covered up for fear of paralyzing research/development enterprises, stands as perhaps most explicit elucidation of this idea.)

The UFO/"alien" phenomenon described by Jacques

Vallee, John Keel, and Whitley Strieber is alarmingly congruent with the CTH. We appear to be interacting with an exceptionally patient intelligence which, despite its advantages over terrestrial science, seems limited by a steadfast refusal to make itself widely known. (Whether this indicates a guiding morality or pragmatic necessity remains to be seen.) Contrary to mainstream expectations, our visitors have opted for a much more gradual form of contact, evidenced both by the often theatrical nature of the apparent vehicles in our skies and by the behavior of the presumed occupants (who seem to enjoy letting us assume they hail from outer space).

I propose that this intelligence has played a significant role in occasionally hastening our species' development as well as keeping us in a periodic "standby" state, rendering us less likely to destroy ourselves. In a way, the human legacy has been scripted to conform to an alien template about which we know little or nothing. But the available historical, mythological and experiential evidence tends to support a largely benevolent *raison d'etre*. Perhaps we're being groomed in preparation for our own Singularity, after which the "others" could have no choice but to deal with us as equals.

If we're dealing with aliens—regardless whether or not they originate in space or on Earth—maybe their clumsy, oblique interactions with us can be explained if they're endowed with intelligence but devoid of sentience. They could have taken an evolutionary route that bypassed awareness entirely, or they could have achieved a form of sentience only to lose it, perhaps by recklessly merging with their machines.

"Ufonauts" are often described as behaving in a military or insect-like manner, even moving in lockstep.

Maybe they're interested in us because we're aware in a way they aren't, and they're determined to acquire our capacity for self-reflective thought in order to communicate with us. In essence, our interaction with the UFO intelligence could be a dialogue with a complex but myopic machine. Maybe "they" have never encountered a species like us and are genuinely baffled—insofar as a distributed computer can be "baffled."

Ardent Singularitarians will doubtlessly point out that our brains are effectively distributed computers, in which case the aliens, if they're here, should possess sentience even if mechanical. But a sophisticated intelligence doesn't necessarily need to be aware of itself to perform a task. If we're observing beings created by someone or something else, sentience might have been deliberately excluded from their repertoire for fear of losing control of a useful tool.

Our visitors seem both wildly sophisticated and limitlessly stupid. If they're collectively lacking what we commonly term "spirit," it might be possible to resolve this seeming paradox.

CHAPTER 7

The Superspectrum

Given that radiation like that used by cellphones can infringe on human consciousness—and I think it's very probable it can—we have to question our role in this emerging electronic ecology. If John Keel is correct, and we share the planet with "ultraterrestrials" who occupy higher realms of an unseen "superspectrum," one wonders if we could be upsetting the superspectral hierarchy by marinating our world in a stew of microwaves.

Conversely, maybe the advent of widespread cell communication is analogous to the role of fungi according to Terence McKenna. Instead of viewing ubiquitous cell towers as intrusive and harmful, maybe we should look at them as totems through which we might communicate with unseen intelligences. (I've always thought it interesting that so many UFO sightings have been witnessed over military installations with advanced radar technology; some alleged UFO occupants have even ventured the idea that radar somehow interferes with the operation of their craft—one proposed explanation for the Roswell incident.)

In any case, there appears to be a link between artificial radiation and "alien" visitors. And since some UFOs possess documented microwave properties, we're left with the possibility that we're only now (inadvertently) acknowledging their arrival. What this means in the long-term is anyone's guess. Maybe, by inundating the skies with our collective voice, we're offering the "ultraterrestrials" a sort of Trojan Horse—a technological substrate through which they can penetrate our reality with unprecedented ease.

I find broadcast towers oddly frightening. Maybe they're not tinfoil-hat scary, but they sound a quiet alarm. We seldom take the time to look up and actually *see* these things—which is perhaps understandable, since they're everywhere: anonymous spurs skewering the clouds and filling the sky with unknown chatter.

If we're evolving faster to meet the demands of an increasingly compromised planet, I suppose it's not out of the realm of possibility that our brains are being forced to adapt to the ubiquitous electromagnetic fog spawned by the telecommunications industry. Maybe some UFOs are a way our minds have developed to make sense of the onslaught of radio and microwave radiation that permeates modern culture. Radio inundation might be ripping holes in the collective unconscious, leaving conspicuous voids to be filled.

Albert Budden has speculated along similar lines; he describes "abductions" as the psyche's way of maintaining identity when faced with acute allergic distress. I'm actually quite interested in the esoteric neurological effects of EM exposure. One of the most original UFO books of the last two decades is *UFOs: Psychic Close Encounters: The Electromagnetic Indictment* by Albert Budden, who hypothesizes that EM "hotspots" can result in a variety of troubling "paranormal" experiences, including evident "hauntings" and—you guessed it—alien abduction. (It's worth remembering that ufologist Jacques Vallee has credited genuine UFOs with emitting microwaves, which may play a similar hallucinogenic role in some close encounters. And debunkers are fond of citing the work of Michael Persinger, whose experiments with EM fields and human subjects suggest a link between the "sense of presence" associated with altered states of consciousness and seismic stress.)

Close encounter witnesses almost invariably describe electromagnetic anomalies both in the presence of UFOs / entities and in mundane surroundings. I'm drawn to the possibility that some abductions are energetic intrusions of some sort, a hypothesis that "nuts and bolts" pundits are likely to deride. Perhaps instead of focusing on recovering memories of events occluded by "missing time," researchers should attempt a comprehensive electrical profile of the witness' nervous system and vicinity.

To my knowledge, the only researcher to undertake a rigorous survey of the electromagnetic environment's impact on the experiencer is Albert Budden, who has come to accept that alien visitation and "hauntings" alike can be attributed to EM "hotspots" interacting with the human brain. Budden's model hinges on the human brain's ability to conjure convincing hallucinatory states. And while there's no doubt the brain can be remotely stimulated to produce otherworldly imagery (through both EM and chemical means), laboratory tests have thus far failed to produce anything comparable to an archetypal "abduction" experience.

This frustrating lack of repeatability in a clinical environment invites the possibility that we're dealing with an external phenomenon of considerable power and complexity. Could we, in fact, be dealing with a form of non-human consciousness that takes the form of plasma?

"I sometimes see these entities during meditation

(eyes barely open, soft focus)," writes Kartott, author of the Postreason blog. "They stand (float) about me, seeming to modulate a field of energy around me (I especially sense their hands, 'combing' the energy). There always seems to be one primary entity, usually right in my face, others are more in the background. I don't get any verbal communication from them."

As this description illustrates, the "Gray" archetype seems to possess the ability to manifest in a "visionary" manner. If so, who's responsible? We could be dealing with a hardwired neurological phenomenon, as argued by researchers like Michael Persinger and Albert Budden. Conversely, recurrent images of the Grays—in varying stages of physicality and in a multitude of contexts—beg the idea that they exist independently of the brain (at least temporarily).

The close encounter literature is rife with accounts in which "abductees," convinced their visitors are flesh-and-blood, encounter their assailants in apparent "out-of-body" and similarly altered states, suggesting that the Grays (and their kin) can maneuver in and out of our ontological framework at will. What might this say about the origin of our visitors (if indeed we're dealing with an externally imposed intelligence)?

Perhaps, instead of hailing from space, the "Grays" emanate from a much closer source. As Whitley Strieber suggests in *Communion*, they could be an unacknowledged aspect of the human psyche and thus indistinguishable from mental aberration. As pioneering consciousness researcher Rick Strassman has shown, the aggressively psychedelic compound DMT can produce tellingly similar encounters, offering the novel idea that our brains can function as receivers or portals. (Ultimately, some of us might serve as nothing less than transportation devices for incorporeal intelligences, which might explain why some individuals seem predisposed to contact and the pageantry of strangeness that often accompanies it.)

I'm reminded of Lovelock's Gaia Hypothesis, in which the planet is effectively a single biological entity. Maybe UFOs and their "occupants" are cast members in some vast planetary drama with no actual role other than perpetuating themselves. UFOs and their accompanying entities might be subconsciously reminding us of the potentially apocalyptic burden we bear as an industrial species, all the while encouraging us (via their apparent technological prowess) that we lessen our environmental signature by migrating into space. Such a scenario compliments the "control system" proposed by Jacques Vallee and suggests a link with the collective unconscious explored by Jung, most notably in *Flying Saucers: A Modern Myth of Things Seen in the Skies*.

But where do they come from? If the UFO phenomenon is generated by Earth itself, perhaps it uses the human nervous system as a kind of operating system. Its enduring physicality argues that it can manipulate consciousness in such a way that individuals can function as unwitting projectors. If so, the study of UFOs might eventually lead to a new understanding of the role of awareness. One day, through careful back-engineering of our own minds, we might employ UFO-like abilities through thought alone—in which case the UFO phenomenon risks becoming obsolete.

But forget the idea of "other dimensions" for a moment. Perhaps Jacques Vallee's proposed "psychic thermostat," while a well-intentioned attempt to reconcile UFO observations with their psychosocial effects, isn't needed to encompass the weirdness of alien visitation.

Forget, also, the idea that aliens are necessarily from space. Instead, let's assume for adventure's sake that we're sharing the planet with a flesh-and-blood offshoot of the human species. As I've tried to demonstrate, the prospect isn't as absurd as it initially seems; indeed, I expect it will seem much less so when we've learned more about our world and our relatively brief tenure here. (It bears mention that eminent primatologist Jane Goodall has defended the scientific search for "Bigfoot," a cryptohominid commonly described as enormous. Assuming a gigantic and purportedly foul-smelling primate can successfully lay low, it may be substantially easier for an intelligent technical society, with a tested capacity for stealth and a full repertoire of disinformation tricks, to dodge our radar.)

Astrophysicists discern black holes—the invisible corpses of collapsed stars—by detecting their gravitational influence on neighboring phenomena. Similarly, the search for extrasolar life hinges on the belief that technological civilizations—regardless how advanced—will necessarily betray their existence via electromagnetic emissions. Freeman Dyson, for instance, has suggested hunting for alien megascale engineering by looking for its distinctive energetic signature.

We can apply the same basic principles to the search for nonhuman intelligences here on Earth. If some UFOs are indeed the work of an indigenous race, we ought to be able to detect the inevitable "signature" it's imprinted on the planet. This confirming evidence can take many forms: anomalous fossils, genetic traces, "mystery" transmissions, and even inexplicable artifacts.

Our technology-driven world is effectively shrinking at a pace that threatens to obliterate remaining wilderness areas. At the same time, we continue to map the continents and oceans (not to mention the surfaces of other planets) with ever-improving instruments. It stands to reason that the CTH is testable. In other words, no matter how addicted to seclusion, a parallel society will eventually betray its existence.

But maybe they don't *want* to be found. Maybe they'd prefer to observe from the balcony, unseen and unsuspected, while we go about our blundering affairs onstage. If so, then they've almost certainly noticed the hazard we pose to their maintained stealth. And while they might be our technological superiors, one couldn't blame them for being at least a little concerned.

Whitley Strieber has remarked that his "visitors," the subject of the best-selling *Communion* and subsequent books that delve into the ufological realm, accomplish their agenda largely through stealth and cunning; their technology, as enviable as it may be, is secondary. Strieber attributes the reduction in his encounters with nonhumans to the fact that he no longer resides in his isolated New York cabin, but in the busy community of San Antonio. Apparently the "visitors" (whoever they are) are daunted by the ubiquity of modern civilization, able to exist among us for only limited periods—and even then assisted by considerable disguise and technical savvy.

In many ways, this would be an appalling predicament for our hypothetical ultraterrestrials. For most of human history they would have enjoyed unimpeded dominance. Humans, without a global media infrastructure, would have been easier to fool (and perhaps to exploit) than we are now. (Or do I err on the side of overconfidence?)

In almost any event, the "others" would have been compelled to misdirect us in order to maintain cultural coherence. I suspect that the prevailing notion that they hail from outer space originates from an overarching disinformation campaign with roots that predate humanity as we know it. For millennia, we've interpreted them according to the disguises they adopt, each tailored to mesh with the given paradigm. Even a cursory overview of world folklore indicates that this ability is extraordinarily well-honed; it may be their most zealously guarded secret.

However, I suggest that our abrupt transformation into a global, intricately networked society poses a grave challenge to what has traditionally been a routine effort. We may be on the threshold of some oblique form of contact; alternatively, this contact may have begun in modern times, marked by the emergence of the contemporary UFO phenomenon and the equally alarming epidemic of so-called "alien abductions."

Jacques Vallee has remarked, somewhat famously, about the possible futility of trying to look behind the curtain; what might we be confronted with? Given the opportunity, could we even comprehend what we're seeing?

Like the origin of the "aliens" themselves, this sense of existential humility may prove to be a clever construct designed to limit our perceptions.

CHAPTER 8

Water World

I watched James Cameron's movie *The Abyss* with a true sense of wonder, realizing that while a sufficiently advanced technology may indeed be indistinguishable from magic, absolute stealth could remain a grave concern even for technologically accomplished species. The oceans are the obvious refuge for ETs who'd prefer to inhabit our planet in relative privacy, and it's probably no coincidence that so many UFOs are reported near large bodies of water.

Bodies of water play a significant role in UFO lore. Craft are seen rising from lakes and oceans; sailors observe remarkable wheels of light rotating beneath the hulls of their boats—the aquatic equivalent to today's accounts of "buzzed" airliners.

The mystery can be traced to the dawn of recognized human society. The Sumerian Oannes myth maintains that civilization itself was a gift from beings who hailed from underwater. Before the detrimental pop-culture impact of Erich von Daniken, champion of untenable "ancient astronaut" theories, none other than Carl Sagan speculated that the Sumerian tale might represent an actual account of a meeting with nonhuman intelligence.

Of course, Sagan had in mind visiting extraterrestrials. Given the contemporary evidence for a nonhuman intelligence on this planet, the Oannes myth might instead represent contact between two very different types of terrestrials. That the Sumerians' enigmatic neighbors were interested in passing along the very concepts that would transform humans into city-dwellers is intriguing in light of Charles Fort's famous contention that we are the property of an intelligence that elects to remain unseen. Maybe, by concentrating large numbers of humans into unprecedentedly small enclaves, the human race was being made more amenable to cryptoterrestrial surveillance.

Equally engaging is the continued interest cryptoterrestrials display in human affairs. From unsolicited health check-ups to warnings of imminent ecological cataclysm, our fellow planetary residents appear deeply concerned about our plight, both as a species and, as some cases suggest, individuals. If our alleged "visitors" originate on some distant planet, this obsessive and long-lived attempt to steer the course of our psychosocial evolution certainly challenges modern thought on what "they" might be up to.

SETI theorists, for example, have cited radio communication as plausible means by which we might be contacted by extraterrestrials. Fortunately, the prospect of interstellar travel has gained a footing among mainstream scientists, challenging prevailing dogma that, for decades, confined hypothetical ETs to their home planetary systems. Some astronomers have even hazarded ways the aliens might betray their existence, from scattered microscopic artifacts to automated construction sites in the Asteroid Belt.

Despite the inexorably warming attitude toward ET visitation, mainstream thinkers still prefer the image of aliens as stealthy, clinical observers. UFOs, with their conspicuously visible antics, shatter this model. Many debunkers attempt, fallaciously, to dismiss the phenomenon precisely because it fails to conform with expectations. If ETs are cool and detached, it doesn't make immediate sense why they would have such a severe stake in our existence. If UFOs themselves seem like chancy evidence of ET visitors, face-to-face encounters with actual occupants—who, moreover, look not unlike us—seem exceptionally surreal.

But if we're instead dealing with *indigenous* beings, it's easier to understand why "aliens" might have cause for alarm. Their intervention throughout history indicates that they need us for reasons that are seldom forthcoming.

If cryptoterrestrials are members of a hive society with access to genetic engineering, I can't help but wonder how they'd go about colonizing the oceans and what, precisely, they might be doing there. If the Sumerian Oannes myth is a true account of interspecies contact, then perhaps they really are our benefactors intent on steering us closer to our full potential. (Although some would argue, not entirely without justification, that hunter-gatherer societies are fundamentally healthier and less environmentally abusive than the urban communities that debuted in Mesopotamia.)

The burning question, to my mind, is *why* an advanced nonhuman intelligence would expend considerable resources to hasten our development. Maybe they're effectively farmers using humans for our genes—a notion in keeping with the "reptilian agenda" promoted by conspiracy extremists. (The alleged aliens described by Bob Lazar supposedly viewed humans as "containers," but whether this term denoted DNA or something transcendent was never satisfactorily explained. Whitley Strieber would argue, compellingly, that the "visitors" cherish us as repositories of what we can only call "souls"; alternatively, Budd Hopkins would insist, perhaps just as compellingly, that we're being harvested to serve a long-term hybridization program.)

When abductees question their captors regarding their agenda, they're usually met with cryptic blurbs. For instance, Whitley Strieber writes that he was told, simply, that his tormentors had a "right" to snatch him from his bed and extract semen. (In recent years Strieber has publicly compared the infamous "rectal probe" to an electrostimulator, a device used to induce ejaculations in livestock. While the implications are frightening, it's at least easier to understand the brevity with which he depicted his abduction in 1987's *Communion*. Unfortunately, the ubiquitous "rectal probe" quickly cemented itself into our cultural fabric, fueling the conviction that Strieber's assailants were dispassionate interstellar scientists with an inordinate interest in stool specimens.)

The many cases in which humans witness "hybrid" beings with human and alien traits call for a reconciliation with ancient contact mythology. If nonhumans are responsible, in part, for maintaining (or catalyzing) the human legacy, it would appear their reasons are more selfish than altruistic. Strangely, their desire for our continued survival—if only for the sake of our genetic material—may have played a substantial role in helping us to avoid extinction during the Cold War, when the UFO phenomenon evolved in our skies (much to the consternation of officialdom). The wave of sightings in 1947, for example, seems calculated to appeal to the collective unconscious in ways deftly explored in Carl Jung's *Flying Saucers*.

Later sighting "flaps" possessed the same sense of theater, eventually leading French astrophysicist Jacques Vallee to suggest that we were in the grips of an existential control system. Well aware of the ETH's gnawing limitations, Vallee postulated a "multiverse" in which the controlling intelligence originated in a parallel reality.

This did away with the need for ET visitors and helped explain the seeming absurdity of close encounters in the 1960s, when the "aliens" were regularly sighted miming the exploits of our own Apollo astronauts. It also offered a new way to address the folkloric theme of nonhuman contact that prevails in disparate cultures, from the Irish Faerie Faith to the Ant People of the Hopi.

According to Vallee and John Keel, the UFO/contact phenomenon was necessarily duplicitous, adept at exploiting the witness's belief system in order to appear comprehensible. In Vallee's view, the UFO intelligence is quite real and manifests itself in order to ensure we conform to some inexplicable ideal—but the "spacecraft," regardless of physical evidence, are ultimately illusions (albeit studiously crafted).

In contrast, the hypothesis put forth here argues that some UFOs are in fact real vehicles. But we're not under siege by anthropomorphic ETs or "goblins from hyperspace"; the beings behind the curtain are eminently tangible. They insinuate themselves into our ontological context not to confuse us but to camouflage themselves. The UFO spectacle takes on the flavor of myth because it *wants* to be discounted. At the same time, knowing that their activities are bound to be seen at least occasionally, the occupants deliberately infuse their appearance with what we might expect of genuine extraterrestrial travelers.

It's a formidable disguise—but it can be pierced.

CHAPTER 9

Underground

The subterranean connection isn't limited to sightings of unknown objects emerging from bodies of water; it seems to play a critical—perhaps central—role in the testimony of many abductees, who describe finding themselves transported into apparent caverns teeming with alien activity.

One of the first contemporary abductees to address seemingly below-ground structures was Betty Andreasson, whose story has been patiently chronicled in several volumes by investigator Raymond Fowler. Andreasson's experiences with apparent ETs is one of the most metaphysically charged abduction narratives on record, filled with marvels that seem to have no purpose other than to elicit emotional reactions from the witness. Despite Fowler's diligence as a reporter, he follows the conventional wisdom, concluding that Andreasson has been the subject of decades-long extraterrestrial interference.

But given the aliens' obvious penchant for elaborate visual metaphor and special effects trickery, it's unclear why Fowler (and like-minded researchers) invoke star-hopping visitors. The abduction experience is far more ambiguous. Upon close inspection, the perceived need for ETs withers, replaced by a thicket of unwelcome questions. The abduction phenomenon thus resolutely denies itself; it is up to us whether to accept this as a deliberate challenge on behalf of the controlling intelligence or to abide by its limitations.

Cryptoterrestrial lore is replete with allusions to underground habitats, subterranean labyrinths navigable only to an enlightened few, and even modern-day below-ground facilities staffed, in part, by government operatives. From Richard Shaver's fancifully paranoid tales of the "Deros" to Bob Lazar's depiction of S-4 (allegedly a supersecret base a stone's throw away from Area 51), the "alien" meme challenges us with the prospect that our world is separated from the other by the merest of partitions . . . and that the CTs are almost as comfortable in our bedrooms and on our roadsides as they are in their own realm.

The image of a "Hollow Earth" populated by beings remarkably like ourselves is by no means new, yet the modern UFO phenomenon has infused it with a newly conspiratorial vigor. Stories of alien bases below the unassumingly bleak surface of the American Southwest surfaced in the wake of the MJ-12 controversy, carving the mythos into irresistible new shapes. In *Revelations*, Jacques Vallee recounts a memorable exchange with the late Bill Cooper and Linda Moulton Howe. Told matter-of-factly about the existence of a sprawling subterranean base near Dulce, New Mexico, Vallee asked his hosts where the presumed aliens disposed of their garbage—a sensible question if one assumes that the "Grays" in question are physical beings burdened with corresponding physical requirements.

Vallee's question is of obvious importance to the cryptoterrestrial inquiry. If we really are sharing the planet with a "parallel" species, searching for underground installations becomes imperative for any objective investigation. Our failure to find any blatant "cities" beneath the planet's surface invites many questions. Could the CTs have colonized our oceans, potentially explaining centuries of bizarre aquatic sightings? Have they intermingled to the point where they're effectively indistinguishable from us? (And, if so, how might such a scattered population summon the resources to stage UFO events?)

Finally, we're forced to consider that at least some CTs have achieved genuine space travel, throwing our definitional framework into havoc. Space-based CTs wouldn't be extraterrestrials in the sense argued by ufological pundits, but they *would* be something engagingly "other," even if the difference separating them from their Earth-bound peers is as substantial as that distinguishing astronauts from humans of more mundane professions.

Still, the prospect of an underground origin beckons with the inexorable logic that colors our most treasured contemporary myths. Given our yawning ignorance of our own planet—especially its oceans, which remain stubbornly mysterious—it remains worthy of consideration. From the lusty politics of Mount Olympus to Shaver's pulp cosmology (complete with telepathic harassment and other ingredients later found in "serious" UFO abduction literature), even a cursory assessment of subterranean mythology indicates a nonhuman presence of surprisingly human dimensions.

This striking familiarity—so unlikely in the case of genuine extraterrestrial contact—meshes with modern occupant reports, which typically depict humanoid beings seen in the context of extraordinary technology. Villas-Boas had sex with a diminutive female who, while strangely mannered, can hardly be termed "alien." The alarming fact that intercourse was possible at all smacks of an encounter between two human beings—an observation routinely dismissed by proponents of the Extraterrestrial Hypothesis, who seem inordinately enamored of Villas-Boas' own conviction that he had been used as breeding stock for a race of apparent space people.

The beings encountered by Betty and Barney Hill seem at least as human when addressed safely outside the confines of ETH dogma; even Betty's dialogue with the "leader" has the nuanced, bantering quality of two strangers attempting to come to grips with a mutual predicament. Indeed, the beings' puzzlement when confronted with dentures tends to argue in favor of the CTH. We might reasonably expect bona fide ET anthropologists to set aside the minor mystery of artificial teeth with clinical detachment; instead, Betty's ability to note her abductors' astonishment (feigned or genuine) detracts from the ETH by indicating a suspiciously human rapport.

Since I began writing about indigenous aliens in early 2006, readers have pointed out parallels with similar esoteric theories (usually involving interdimensional travel of some sort). To be fair, the cryptoterrestrial prospect isn't as new as it might seem to readers new to forteana. This was struck home upon encountering the work of William Michael Mott, a researcher enamored of mythological tales of lost civilizations and underground habitats. His book *Caverns, Cauldrons, And Concealed Creatures* suggests that there is very strong circumstantial evidence—based on folklore, mythology, religion, archeology, geology, history and also on eyewitness and anecdotal accounts— that indicates that we have always shared our planet with one or more hidden civilizations of an advanced nature, which are generally inimical, parasitical, or indifferent to humanity.

Is it feasible that the alleged aliens that occupy historical and contemporary mythology are flesh-and-blood human-like creatures that live right here on Earth? Not another version of Earth in some parallel Cosmos, but *our* Earth.

A lynchpin of the CTH is that at least some of the more remarkable abilities displayed by reported aliens are in fact subterfuge—immersive fictional scenarios staged to convince us we must be dealing with beings from another star system. Vallee and Keel have, of course, argued much the same thing. But both have maintained (unnecessarily, in my opinion) that the beings must hail from somewhere else—not outer space, but an unseen realm that makes the outer space option seem *almost* preferable.

Needless to say, today's ufological pundits have decided to stick with the ETH. Sure, it's weird and by no means offers a holistic understanding of the phenomenon it purports to explain, but at least it makes sense in light of our own technological trajectory. After all, *we've* visited space (albeit briefly); the ETH has the overall appearance of a logical extrapolation.

The CTH is a synthesis. In keeping with the "nuts and bolts" tradition, it incorporates what we know about our planet and its biology and arrives at a prospective anthropology of the "other." It eschews interstellar travel in favor of beings that may not be nearly as alien as we've been conditioned to expect—by the media and (as I argue) by the UFO intelligence itself.

The Cryptoterrestrial Hypothesis has met with mixed reactions. Some Forteans seem to think I'm onto something. Most UFO researchers are, at best, extremely skeptical.

Others think I'm parroting John Keel's "superspectrum," a variation on the "parallel worlds" theme that in turn shares memes with Jacques Vallee's "multiverse." Both ideas suggest that we somehow occupy dimensional space with our "alien" visitors, doing away with the need for extraterrestrial spacecraft while helping explain the sense of absurdity that accompanies many UFO and occupant sightings.

Keel and Vallee have both ventured essentially "occult" ideas in cosmological terms; both the "superspectrum" and the "multiverse" require a revision of our understanding of the way reality itself works. But the Cryptoterrestrial Hypothesis is grounded in a more familiar context; I'm not suggesting unseen dimensions or the need for ufonauts to "downshift" to our level our consciousness. And while I can't automatically exclude the UFO phenomenon's "paranormal" aspects, I *can* attempt to explain them in technological terms. (For example, I see no damning theoretical reason why "telepathy" and "dematerialization" can't ultimately be explained by appealing to cybernetics, nanotechnology, and other fields generally excluded from ufological discourse.)

Ironically enough, the CTH manages to alienate champions of the ETH *and* those who support a more esoteric, "interdimensional" explanation. It offers no clearcut reconciliation. It does, however, wield explanatory potential lacking in both camps.

One question that hasn't escaped me is how, if we're sharing the planet with indigenous "aliens," the worsening of the biosphere will impact any potential relationship with our secretive neighbors. If they're physical, as I think they are, they stand to suffer greatly if (for example) a human-induced climate disaster sets the Amazon rainforest ablaze . . . or do they?

Perhaps the cryptoterrestrials have taken precautionary measures. Persistent reports of underground bases raise the admittedly alarming possibility that the CTs are subterranean. Even descriptions of the beings themselves almost invariably include reference to large eyes—which proponents of the Extraterrestrial Hypothesis interpret as an evolutionary advantage for life on planets with diminished sunlight. But large eyes would be equally useful for beings acclimated to tunnels and caverns. Maybe the CTs, having constructed effective "bunkers," are content to let humans continue in their heedless destruction of the planet.

But then there are the scenes of global cataclysm shown to abductees. Some researchers are understandably wary of viewing these as literal forecasts of the future and see them instead as educational demonstrations. If so, it's plausible that the CTs are attempting to hasten ecological awareness—and in the process giving away a grave secret: that they aren't the sagely, omniscient beings whose role they so often adopt. Their technological wizardry might *not* be akin to magic. They might actually need us to keep Earth's environment sustainable just as they may need us for our genes—and likely for the same ultimate reason: the cultivation of an ever-adaptive race whose abilities are beyond our own yet perfectly fallible.

Gray aliens on the brain? That's likely what you'll get.

That's not to say the Grays are the only comprehensible form instigated by "faery energy"—only that the ambient intelligence is quick to attach itself to whatever archetype fits the bill at any given moment. Visions of dead people, religious epiphanies, and poltergeist phenomena are equally possible outcomes.

But the intelligence behind the facade *might not be native to our planet*; maybe we're dealing with a psychological symbiote that's been re-engineering the noosphere for hundreds of thousands of years, laying groundwork for a project that's only know beginning to reveal itself . . .

While I can readily imagine a subterranean civilization of nonhumans, I find the idea that intelligent beings could *evolve* there unlikely. Secluding themselves in underground "bases" might be a relatively recent event, timed to avoid a mutually catastrophic run-in with *Homo sapiens*.

Caverns and tunnels repeatedly crop up in the alien contact literature. Witnesses sometimes describe lavish below-ground installations teeming with beings that may or may not be related to humans. This is certainly compatible with the idea that our "visitors" have been here at least as long as recorded history, spared the toxic excesses of known civilization. In effect, they could inhabit an immense fallout shelter, having foreseen our own demise and taken elaborate precautions.

The apparent need for genetic material might indicate the creation of an interim "occupying force" of passable hybrids, a scenario explored in David Jacobs' *The Threat*.

The CTH doesn't necessarily entail a global civilization of nonhumans. In fact, I find the possibility that the cryptoterrestrials have managed to remain socially intact throughout the millennia especially tenuous. Witness reports and common sense alike point toward a more likely scenario: that the CTs are wildly variant, at different levels of sophistication. While in possession of remarkable abilities—not the least of which is the capacity for stealth—some CT communities might even qualify as "primitive" in some respects.

Some CTs appear eminently comfortable among technologies that, historically, seem just beyond the human state-of-the-art. The pilots of the "mystery airships" of the 1890s, for example, seemed to have anticipated our own dominion of the air at least as capably as Jules Verne. Betty Hill's eerily accurate description of amniocentesis has been cited as another case of "alien" technology seen in action before its widespread implementation in the human realm. Again, this isn't what we would expect of an arbitrarily capable extraterrestrial civilization. Rather, it suggests a technology surprisingly like our own, another indication that the beings' casual allusions to outer space should be taken with a dose of healthy skepticism. (Although we shouldn't presume that some CTs haven't succeeded in gaining a foothold in space, making them a novel kind of ET. Maybe the term "post-terrestrial" best describes this offshoot.)

Unfortunately, reports of technologically savvy entities have all-but eclipsed equally credible reports of less sophisticated beings. After all, advanced beings promise a welcoming future, if only indirectly. If we should detect a genuine extraterrestrial civilization, whether through an instrumented search like SETI or via direct visitation, hopes for our own continued existence stand to reap enormous rewards. Consequently, we yearn for "others" who are both wiser and more capable.

The attractive human-like "aliens" who contacted the likes of George Adamski and Howard Menger in the middle of the 20th century were hailed as veritable messiahs, their disdain for reckless atomic experimentation reiterated in the fiction of the day. To a somewhat lesser extent, today's Grays—though harsher and more pragmatic than their glamorous predecessors—convey the same message, exposing their subjects to scenes that appear to predict impending apocalypse.

In a world suffering from pronounced greenhouse effects and record-breaking extinctions, these images couldn't come at a more opportune time. Either the CTs are studiously exploiting our deepest fears as part of some far-ranging psychological experiment or their concerns are quite real. But is it our world they care about or their own? The existence of "primitive" CT communities leaves us no choice but to willfully deflate our confidence in the Extraterrestrial Hypothesis—especially when the gross resemblances of the alleged ETs to humans are so pronounced.

For example, I have a reliable first-hand report of "little people" at large in the American Northwest. My source encountered a small congregation of these beings in a wooded area. Human-like in all essential respects, the beings were nevertheless small, like normal people in miniature. Although the encounter was brief, my source was able to glean some important information. The "little people" claimed to predate known North American cultures and possessed their own language. As in so many other accounts of meetings with ufonauts or "paranormal" entities, they appeared Asian, again inviting speculation that they originate from a "lost" community that has opted for a peripheral role, effectively hidden from the mainstream.

According to the beings' spokesman, they remain hidden largely by virtue of our narrow perceptual focus, even able to pass among us disguised as children. Supposedly they lead an almost hobo-like existence, without recourse to the sort of technology associated with UFOs.

While this all sounds innocuous enough, my source qualified his story by stating that he felt that his meeting had been arranged not so much for his benefit as for *theirs*—an unsettling idea that brings to mind a surveillance program of potentially epic scope. Abductees sometimes report visits by curious human-seeming interlopers, or even symptoms consistent with electronic eavesdropping (up to and including so-called "implants," but just as often strange hissing on the telephone or the sudden onset of "electrosensitivity," rendering witnesses unable to operate delicate electronics). One abductee I know is plagued by seemingly sourceless beeping—a phenomenon encountered as early as the famous Hill abduction.

If I'm correct and "down to Earth" cryptoterrestrials and "ETs" are aspects of the same phenomenon, we should expect certain parallels. Moreover, we should never believe what the others tell us without taking into account their obvious need for secrecy. One may argue that the mere fact that they initiate open contact with humans at all reeks of misdirection, and perhaps that's the point. But they could just as easily genuinely need a network of human contacts, a foothold in our world to fall back on in times of crisis.

If nomadic CTs are forced to adopt a marginal role in our world, it's unlikely they have easy access to the communications infrastructure we take for granted; maybe it's no coincidence that my source is a computer programmer. Or the truth could be markedly less conspiratorial. Maybe they simply crave a sympathetic ear. And if they can successfully masquerade as children and homeless people, why exclude the occasional "pop-in" visit?

CHAPTER 10

Among Us

I'm drawn to first-person stories of perceived encounters with nonhumans. Among them, I found this recollection by Kartott especially notable:

… when I was 17, I was working in a small convenience store, when a "woman" came in to buy cigarettes. At first I didn't pay any attention to her until I saw her hand (when she handed me the money)—it was not like a normal human hand. This startled me so I looked up and saw a very pale entity, wearing a thin black coat (like a rain coat) with collar turned up to cover her neck, a heavy long haired wig, and very large black glasses. This did not entirely hide her strange face: a very pointed chin, scant lip and nose. She did not speak. Took her cigarettes and left! I was kinda stunned. Oddly I cannot remember the details of her hand (though it was the first thing I noticed). Nor do I think she left in a car which was odd since most patrons drove up the store (it was somewhat isolated).

Kartott provided more details of the cigarette lady in a later post:

….whether this entity is a "gray" or a "hybrid," I can only guess. I have never seen what is described as a classic gray

alien. Perhaps "hybrid" is most fitting simply because there seems to be some variety of attributes associated with this general category; i.e. that do not fit perfectly with the classic gray alien type (size of head being foremost).

Some details that I do recall with some clarity:

First, her skin: it was very pale, white with an almost bluish-gray tint to it, and of an unusually smooth texture. I have never seen anything like it before or since. I had previously seen an albino person; it was nothing like that; i.e., her skin was not UN-pigmented though there was an almost translucent quality to it.

Second, her facial features: Though I could not see her eyes due to the large Jackie-O style sunglasses she wore, other aspects were evident: an unusually long pointy chin. Exaggerated cheekbones out of proportion to the rest of the face. Practically no lips, only enough to discern that there was any mouth. A nose that was almost not there: there was very little structure to it, a small bridge area, and some structure around the nostrils, but not much.

Finally, her neck: though her coat collar was turned up, I could see some of the neck which was oddly thin.

The wig (obviously such: a long thick dishwater blonde mane made of cheap imitation hair easily obtainable at a k-mart in those days) seemed placed to hide other features of the head, so I cannot comment on these (ears, shape of head).

It puzzles me why I cannot recall her hand. Perhaps because it was what most startled me at first. The only thing I can relate to this lack of recall to is a nasty car accident I had years later: afterwards I completely blanked out the memory of the worst part of the accident (the part when it was occurring). I asked my doctor about this and was told that it was not uncommon for the human brain to "forget" traumatic or difficult events. I can only surmise the initial part of the encounter with the cigarette lady falls into this category.

There were no other people in the store. I was alone. It was afternoon. The year of this encounter was 1974, possibly 1975 (I worked both summers between high school and college, and

between my 1st and 2nd years of college); but most likely 1974.
The location was an area south of St. Louis, Missouri. I felt
no lingering psychological effect from this encounter that I am
aware of, other than extreme puzzlement (and the blocked mem-
ory of her hand). As to whether this changed me, I don't know

Consciously or not, Kartott is describing a being strik-
ingly similar to the woman supposedly encountered by
abductee Antonio Villas Boas. Indeed, the pointed chin,
exaggerated cheekbones and vestigial nose and mouth
are commonly reported characteristics of ostensibly
"alien" entities and crop up with compelling frequency in
the UFO literature. The visage has become synonymous
with that of the "Gray," a commonly portrayed UFO occupant type with massive black eyes and fetal characteristics. (The Grays are often described as sexless or even
robotic, stirring discussion that they're in fact biological
robots or even genetically atrophied human time-travel-
ers from our own ecologically impoverished future.)

Although the being described by Villas Boas is perhaps the most obvious example of an apparently alien
woman, one has to look no further than the cover of
Whitley Strieber's iconic 1987 best-seller *Communion* for
another. (Often assumed to depict a male extraterrestrial,
the text of *Communion* and subsequent books by Strieber
emphasizes that the being on the book's cover is female.)

In a disquieting twist, researchers have noted a conspicuous resemblance between the *Communion* alien and
"Lam," the "magickal" entity allegedly summoned by
controversial occultist Aleister Crowley. Like Strieber's
female contact and Villas Boas' seductress, Lam's portrait
emphasizes a memorably tapered face with dramatically
pointed chin and minimal nose and mouth, suggesting a
common origin. (At least some of the infamous "Men In
Black" would also seem to fit the mold.)

Kartott's "cigarette lady" seems to fit the pattern.
Even the purchase of cigarettes—however seemingly pre-
posterous—is in keeping with reports by self-proclaimed

abductees, who have described the smell of cigarette smoke in the context of their encounters. (The distinctively repellent odor of sulfur is a more common variant, with both mythological and folkloric antecedents.)

I propose—tentatively—that the beings featured in this encounter are "alien" only in the sense that they seem exceedingly strange to us. Their predominantly humanoid manner and ability to function in "normal" human reality—if fleetingly—argue that they're denizens of our own planet. Perhaps they're materializations of the sort postulated by John Keel in such books as *The Mothman Prophecies* and *The Eighth Tower*.

Of course, the unmistakably elfin qualities described by UFO witnesses suggest Jacques Vallee's heretical notion of a "multiverse" inhabited by all manner of humanoid intelligences, a hypothesis that begs a scientific analysis of unlikely "contact" reports attributed to indigenous beings such as fairies.

Alternatively, liminal beings like Kartott's cigarette woman might represent a race of human-alien "hybrids," as argued by Budd Hopkins and David Jacobs. Apparently unable to pass among us for great lengths of time, the hybrids' overseers might be content to allow their creations to practice certain basic social skills in a relatively unbounded setting.

Of course, the answer could be a fusion of any of the above possibilities . . . or we could be dealing with a phenomenon generated at least partly by the psyche. The supposed aliens that witnesses see within and outside of UFOs might be examples of what Dr. John Mack termed "reified metaphor"—a physical intrusion of repressed archetypal forces. If so, it's all-too-tempting to speculate that the daimonic reality traditionally accessed by shamanic cultures has begun to spill over into waking consciousness, manifesting as a veritable onslaught of beings quietly seeking to reassert their influence.

In a mechanistic society, the "Other" might find itself faced with extinction; violations of restricted airspace and face-to-face encounters with unsuspecting observers could amount to a kind of existential assertion, begging the possibility that our capacity for belief is somehow integral to our visitors' reality . . . if, indeed, "visitors" is the proper term.

In *Transformation*, Whitley Strieber's follow-up to his best-selling *Communion*, he relates an unusual encounter between Bruce Lee, a colleague in the publishing business, and two "people" with their faces obscured by scarves, hats, and sunglasses.

The beings, short in stature, were rapidly thumbing through copies of *Communion* and commenting on it. Intrigued, Lee asked them what they thought of the book, which had just hit bookshelves. Only then did he notice that, despite attempts to conceal their features, they appeared not unlike the iconic "Gray" featured on *Communion*'s cover.

I once asked Strieber about this incident in an online chat, curious if the beings Lee had supposedly seen were big-eyed Grays or more human-like, perhaps fitting the general description of "hybrids." Strieber insisted the people in the bookstore were identical to the creature on the cover of *Communion*; further, he was convinced Lee had told him the truth. Strieber added that he had personally seen human-looking beings working with the Grays, but didn't elaborate. Given his more recent musings on the nature of the abduction experience, one is left to wonder if the humans seen in the midst of apparent nonhumans are themselves alien in some crucial respect—or else nonhuman beings in exceptionally clever disguises.

Of course, many dismiss Strieber. Some of his assertions, while governed by a curious internal logic, seem too outlandish—or simply too frightening—to conscience. But similar episodes have been recounted by others. Taken together, these accounts paint a bizarre picture of "aliens" in our midst—some predominantly humanoid in appearance, others conforming to the "Gray" archetype.

Regularly described as frail or even sickly, these little-remarked visitors play a quiet but important role in the cryptoterrestrial agenda. They behave skittishly, as if painfully aware of the possibility of detection. Paradoxically, they can also act with surprising confidence, establishing a deep rapport with "normal" humans . . . and disappearing just as mysteriously. Like the fairies of Celtic mythology, these "emissaries" are enticingly *liminal*, at once worldly and wary. While they seem entirely physical, their home turf seems to be a Keelian interzone, as if their passport to our domain forever hovers on the verge of expiration.

Despite differences in appearance, commonly reported traits suggest a common origin. Cryptoterrestrials, like the Grays typically encountered in altered states or aboard evident vehicles, tend to have long fingers, pointed chins and large heads. Their complexion, usually pale or ashen, has also been described as olive or even sunburned. Perhaps most revealingly, their eyes are almost always described as slanted and Asian-like, begging the possibility that, in an abstruse way, they *are* Asian, perhaps descendants of some lost colony that diverged from the genetic mainstream tens of thousands of years ago. Ever-reclusive, their successors may thrive below-ground or beneath bodies of water. (Geologists sometimes complain, with justified exasperation, that we know more about the surface of the Moon than the topology of our home planet.)

Incidentally, the "little people" of folklore are regularly sighted emerging from underground communities—a thread that we rediscover among recent accounts of alien abduction and even the enduring conspiracy lore of the

American Southwest, where spindly beings from Zeta Reticuli are said to have established subterranean cities in conjunction with human scientists.

Visitation from the sky is at least as common. In *The Invisible College*, Jacques Vallee points out that all known creation myths involve beings from above. Anthropologists attribute this to our innate fascination with the Cosmos just above our heads, which plays such a pivotal role in the formation and sustained existence of our communities. But it's just as possible that some of these mythical accounts stem from actual encounters with airborne "gods," posing the notion that the crypto-terrestrials, despite their maddening ambiguity and disciplined stealth, may view themselves as our benefactors.

Indeed, ancient accounts of nonhuman intervention throw the modern spectacle of UFO abductions and sightings of humanoids into a disorienting light; while to all appearances it's the "others" in dire need of *us*, there's at least some reason to think we owe our existence to *them*. As we continue to sort through the subterfuge and misdirection, we find ourselves in a troublingly Escher-like territory, our own genetic legacy abruptly lost in the depths.

We find ourselves treading an existential ledge, wondering what role we ultimately play. The trite dichotomy of "humans" and "aliens" is revealed as inadequate; the truth is metamorphic, and so ancient that our co-existence with indigenous humanoids has become oddly invisible, a secret kept just out of conscious reach.

If the cryptoterrestrials are real and indeed "living among us" (or at least secluded in enclaves), they must have a sense of ethics, a guiding morality. Or at least it's comforting to think so.

The simple fact that they haven't taken over the planet could be proof that they harbor no genocidal grudge. But it could just as easily mean that they need us, either for our genes or for esoteric reasons. But this kicks up its own share of questions.

If they're underpopulated and need humans to refresh their gene-pool, forsaking secrecy and claiming the planet on their own terms would allow their population to expand to viable proportions. We'd no longer be needed. So why are we allowed to continue to exist? By almost any ecological standard, we're terrible neighbors. Do they feel sorry for us? Are they convinced that, through careful psychological engineering, they can improve our "relationship" (albeit without our consent), thus steering the biosphere from the brink of collapse?

Or are they even now eyeing our endeavors with mounting alarm and suspicion? Will there ever come a point that brings the CTs out of hiding—if only to turn the tables on their uneasy truce with our civilization?

Perhaps they'd like to but can't. The evidence suggests they're accomplished illusionists and insidiously clever strategists endowed with abilities once ascribed to the domain of magic. But they give little indication of violence, at least in a military sense. Perhaps their technology, remarkable as it is, isn't conducive to the kind of effort required to invade and conquer; indeed, with our nuclear missiles and arsenal of "black ops" aircraft, we might pose a considerable threat to them. Like the vampires in Whitley Strieber's *The Hunger*, the CTs might be a race in decline. Stealth, it seems, comes with a price: the lack of infrastructure we take for granted.

Maybe the CTs have no real plans for overt colonization. We tend to project our own tendencies onto "aliens"; if we were in their place, we'd inevitably feel subjugated, even claustrophobic. Inevitably, at least some of us would choose to fight back, even if our efforts were desperate and feeble. But the CTs remain strangely pacifist. Either they really are at the mercy of our omnipresent postin-dustrial society or they have plans in store that we have yet to discern.

In *The Threat*, David Jacobs argues that alien hybrids will ultimately reign, with humans reduced to a second-ary role. One could reasonably argue that the CTs are waging a long-term war of attrition, slowly but methodi-cally creating an army of hybrids to inherit and transform the human world. But folkloric evidence begs us to look in other directions. If "they" merely wanted the planet they could have taken it from us long ago, before the in-vention of doomsday weapons and modern surveillance technology. Instead, they seem to have left us to take our own route—or at least leave us with this impression.

Given that they're content to remain marginal, we must consider that we're more than a reserve of DNA. The CTs must have other, less pragmatic, motives. Witness ac-counts offer tantalizing hints that the CTs are at least as intrigued by our minds as they are dependent on our genes. If so, we could be more than we think we are.

The CTs could be reaping an invisible harvest grown in the fertile soil of Mind itself. Limited to short-term agendas and materialistic obsessions, we wouldn't neces-sarily notice. But if the CTs' penchant for psychodrama persists through the next century—and so far it shows no signs of stopping—we just might catch a more expansive look at their goals.

But will we like what we see?

CHAPTER 11

Final Thoughts

Greg Bishop posits that brushes with the paranormal, just like encounters with genuine art, convey meaning by remaining purposefully elusive. My own creative powers (such as they are) suffer when I try to adhere to a template, which is one of the reasons I try to keep away from writing "how-to" texts, as seductive as some of them are. But when I relax my guard—never an easy trick—I find that meaning and structure often arise as if of their own volition.

The field of ufology suffers from a related problem, the toxic assumption that UFOs and other elements of forteana must necessarily yield to a single consciously derived explanation—whether the hallowed Extraterrestrial Hypothesis or something else.

I'd argue that Budd Hopkins' insistence that the small, white-skinned entities are literal "aliens" is as lamentably simple-minded as Susan Clancy's own wholesale ignorance of the abduction enigma as portrayed in her book, *Abducted: How People Come to Believe They Were Kidnapped by Aliens.* "Aliens in jumpsuits" may simply be how the modern Western mind reacts to a "reality-transforming" stimulus.

In a similar manner, explaining the beings as ancestral ghosts could be equally valid. In each case, the mind accesses a comprehensible psychic vocabulary to describe an event that may defy empirical analysis.

This isn't to say Hopkins is wrong; perhaps we really are dealing with more-or-less comprehensible biped aliens with white skin and a penchant for shiny jumpsuits. But the UFO encounter evidence has roots that go far deeper than the contemporary infatuation with "abductions." When the phenomenon is examined historically, it seems more likely that the "aliens" insinuate themselves into a given cultural matrix by appealing to ready-made mythological constructs—thus the near-endless procession of elves, dwarves, fairies, and saucer-pilots that haunt our attempts to discern the "other."

I think someone is here. But to ascribe nonhuman visitation to Hopkins' meddling intruders is to play into a long-standing perceptual trap . . . and the toll might not be merely intellectual.

If we're dealing with a truly alien intelligence, there's no promise that its thinking will be linear. Indeed, its inherent weirdness might serve as an appeal to an aspect of the psyche we've allowed to atrophy. It might be trying to rouse us from our stupor, in which case it's tempting to wonder if the supposed ETs are literally us in some arcane sense.

I alternate between grave misanthropy and chomping-at-the-bit optimism. If the human species is destined to fail—wiped out by its own toxic excesses or slaughtered by warfare—I see no real point in continuing; an extraterrestrial biologist could argue that we're simply taking up time in which the planet could excrete a new biosphere from which a more promising intelligence might arise.

But of course we don't know where we're headed. So we make educated forecasts and hope that our warnings are heeded before it's too late. All too often this seems like an exercise in futility. Sometimes I fear that we've reached a critical threshold, that the human population will be decimated before we can ensure a meaningful, abundant world for ourselves and our descendants (who may well not be human in the contemporary sense). For Earth and its teeming billions of passengers, the end is always nigh; for too long we've relied on blind luck and narrow escapes. Despite brushes with cataclysm and the rigors of evolution, we've survived—but only barely.

Although I harbor serious reservations about humanity's ability to make the evolutionary cut, I'm not without hope. I sense great things in the making. I enjoy experiencing this dire, ever-accelerating point in our species' history; our potential as genuine cosmic citizens challenges the imagination and stretches conceptual boundaries to dizzy extremes.

I'm willing to embrace transcendence or endure extinction. I must perpetually concede either possibility, no matter how dramatically different, regardless of how exciting or dismal. I walk a fine existential edge, fearing and cherishing, enlivened by a vertiginous sense of astonishment and horror.

Afterword

Mac Tonnies was a kindred spirit and an inspiration to me because he always seemed to be able to express difficult and exciting concepts in an eloquent manner. In his quiet, but insistent way, Mac was also metaphorically smacking UFO researchers in the back of the head, asking them to consider an idea that is so old that it's new: What if "aliens" aren't from other planets?

The extraterrestrial belief that has a stranglehold on many of us will loosen its grip when popular views of physics and perception move away from the late 19th century models that have dominated them for so long. When "now" becomes the "everywhen," and we fully absorb the implications of the effect of the observer on the observed and our complicity in the continuous creation of our reality, UFOs and other paranormal phenomena may hold less mystery for us. *The Cryptoterrestrials* is one of the first boulders hurled at the modern citadel of entrenched conventional wisdom.

This book is reaching us at the right time. Perhaps the worst thing about Mac's tragic early death at age 34 is the realization that there were so many more books he was going to write—not all on UFOs and non-humans, but speculative titles delving deeply into the connections between science fiction, futurism, cutting-edge science, and the paranormal, and how they affect each other and therefore our popular views on the unexplained. He immersed himself in these subjects and found insight, which he passed on to readers.

The Cryptoterrestrials could do for the paranormal what Colin Wilson's 1958 volume *The Outsider* did for modern philosophy: ask the difficult questions and offer insights that almost no one had thought of. Wilson dealt with the inner workings of the creative mind; Tonnies surfs modern ideas about UFOs and "aliens" and probes the tributaries that most others prefer to ignore. If this book can cause a tempest in the teacup that is "ufology," then perhaps it can spill over into the mainstream culture.

It might take the world a little while to catch up. Mac admits early on that his proposal is anything but modest and is almost guaranteed to turn off both the seasoned UFO chaser and the casual dilettante. This volume is probably not for the uninitiated, or those who don't accept the idea that we are interacting in some way with something that is not us. Once we allow this as a serious possibility, a whole host of questions rear their scary heads. Mac used this as a working hypothesis, but since he was not a card-carrying paranormal researcher, he was never anointed by the UFO cognoscenti, and he most assuredly didn't care.

In our conversations, he never once mentioned any involvement in a nighttime "UFO watch," nor had he interviewed a UFO witness and filed a report, or critically questioned an abduction researcher. For many, this brings up the scary specter of "armchair research," the bugaboo of ET believer and skeptic alike. We spoke on a few occasions about the as-yet unchristened discipline of "theoretical ufology" and how this should not be considered a derisive term.

Perhaps the main purpose of *The Cryptoterrestrials* is to encourage the fermentation of ideas. I wrote a commentary on this subject for the *UFO Mystic* blog recently:

This method [theoretical discourse] is of course well established in other, more conventional disciplines as a way of pushing research into new areas. Perhaps one of the best examples is in the area of physics, where theory often has real-world applications. Of course the study of UFOs is not a science, but methods of reaching for new knowledge applies here too. The fact that no one has come to any verifiable conclusions about the subject in over fifty years should make some realize that the pain will stop once we stop banging our heads on the wall.

The complaint that many of the old guard (and some of the

new) level against theories without field work may be wearing
thin. Many theories come into being by observing and collating
data. Some of the more robust ideas are further backed up by
repeatable results. Since we cannot do this with UFO sightings,
we are left to sift data that has been painstakingly collected over
many years.

Don't think for a minute that Tonnies believed
wholeheartedly in what you read here. His speculation
is sincere. His thoughts are well reasoned. But he was not
ready to latch on to any theories (even his own) to the ex-
clusion of others. In the UFO field, those who do are guaranteed to look like fools sooner or later. Tonnies adopted
this attitude not to avoid ridicule, but because it appears
to be the only sane approach. This book is an honest pursuit of ideas that might lead to some greater understanding of the paranormal and the existence of an apparent
non-human intelligence. The concepts expressed herein
will germinate in new generations of UFO students, as
thinkers like John Keel, Jacques Vallee, Jim Brandon, and
even Whitley Strieber kindled new ideas in us. If there is a
dividing line between the old and new in this field, Mac's
last book highlights that line with a fluorescent glow.

The time in which Mac Tonnies came of age arrived
when I was well into my 30s. In college, I did research in
libraries and typed my term papers on an IBM PC Junior
with a whopping 64 kilobytes of random access memory and a nimble processor speed of 3.5MHz (my basic
Macintosh now runs 4,500 times faster and cost me much
less). In many ways, I am dangerously close to being a
dinosaur. Mac moved in the world of cyberspace as a native, and his thinking was forged in the more abstract and
nonlocal popular logic of the last decade. He taught this
postmodern language to me in our many phone and internet conversations, as well as on the few occasions that
I was lucky enough to hang out with him.

This is why *The Cryptoterrestrials* will find its most
lasting home amongst generations Y and Z—in an age

where numerous "experts" have lost their halos after getting it wrong so many times, or in the loud denial of a phenomenon which continues to assert itself through reports from thousands of sincere and often educated witnesses from all over the world.

Blinded by the stark black-and-white of witness testimony (often procured with leading and narrow questions), researchers are often working under the assumption that with UFOs, what you see is what you get, and damn the anomalous data that doesn't fit the ET mold. Many excite themselves with what I refer to as "UFO porno"—sighting reports, government documents, and the occasional out-of-focus video. The majority of purveyors and consumers of these artifacts are not really interested in any answers. They already have one. With no commonly accepted proof to back up their claims, they already know that it's aliens from outer space. That attitude is not necessarily wrong, but it is incredibly limiting.

We have no solid answers to the UFO puzzle and those who realize that fact should be excited by new ideas. While some might dismiss Mac Tonnies' writings as "psychological mumbo-jumbo," the inquiring and circumspect among us should take his arguments under serious advisement. Evolution does not come to a reverent halt simply because a generation wants to think that they are at (or nearly at) the venerated end of a long search for the "truth." Prejudices blur our view, and we should be aware of this while in pursuit of a phenomenon that seems to take advantage of our emotional responses.

The Cryptoterrestrials asks us to consider the role that we play in creating our UFO myths. We might perceive the ufonauts as kindly, since the "invasion" appears benign to us, in the sense that it does not affect the daily lives of most people. These intrusions might be affected in a way that is so subliminal that our psychological and cultural overlay is virtually all that remains in thousands of reports of "aliens" and "UFOs," with only a slight whisper of the real source left to puzzle us. Whether this comes from outer space or closer to home, it could be what an intelligence outside our own may do to introduce themselves, or are perhaps attempts to do so time after time over millennia. The UFO "reality" is probably co-creation. Our cultural background and expectations combined with the phenomenon itself produces a result that is more than the sum of its parts, and many of us continue to insist on looking at the finger rather than where it may be pointing.

For the generic UFO researcher and most of the public, the extraterrestrial hypothesis is that comforting finger. It flatters our prejudices and extrapolates neatly from concepts embedded deeply in western culture from at least the early 20th century. The meme may have been planted perhaps as far back as 1727, when Jonathan Swift wrote *Gulliver's Travels*, which described a race of beings obsessed with mathematics who live on a flying island called Laputa. In 1892, Australian Robert Potter produced a novel entitled *The Germ Growers*, which described a stealth invasion by aliens who make themselves appear human and develop a disease to wipe out the dominant species. Six years later, H.G. Wells published *War Of The Worlds*. Wells actually contemplated an alternate ending to his story concerning a future where humans move underground to conduct a generations-long guerilla war against the conquering Martians, much as Mac proposes in this volume, albeit with *Homo sapiens* playing the part of the "invaders" and the crypto-race fighting for survival in the face of encroaching modernity.

One of Mac's favorite authors was Charles Fort, compiler of strange natural anomalies who famously wrote "I think we're property" in his *Book Of The Damned*, which reached astonished readers in 1919. Fort speculated that at least some of the witnessed phenomena he culled from scientific journals and the popular press of his time could be ascribed to a vast intelligence which existed outside of contemporary concepts of reality, and whose machinations appeared absurd from our point of view. Fort imagined a godlike entity that messed with humanity for its own ends and perhaps even for amusement. Later in the century, after decades of sightings and close encounter cases, we have devolved into narrowly bifurcated discussions of evil or benevolent space visitors. It seems that we have not kept pace with our expected intellectual evolution.

At the dawn of the 21st century, advances in nanotechnology allow us to speculate on devices so small that almost infinite numbers of them could invade and change our world undetected. The garden-variety UFO researcher usually ignores this tributary in favor of flashy ships from Zeta Reticuli. As Tonnies writes: "While scintillating 'spaceships' and irradiated landing sites are certainly cause for wonder and scientific concern, they appear suspiciously mired in the science fantasies of the previous century." Mac is extrapolating here with postmodern technology and insights, breaking free of the old science-fiction model that has mired the study of UFOs for so long.

One month before his death, Mac was a guest on the popular *Coast to Coast* radio show, reaching an audience of millions. He sounded at ease and confident in his opinions, and presented himself and his ideas like a pro: clearly and simply. After he went off the air, I called to offer post-interview encouragement and to hear what he thought about his appearance. In contrast to what I expected, he was thrilled with the experience and humble in its afterglow, with little of the self-doubt I expected based on his feelings about his past media exposure. The hell of it now is that he was poised to become the one of the most eloquent spokesman for a new popularization of the anti-ET school.

On reading Mac's last book, what we are left with is a mind cutting through much of the self-satisfied, bloated fundamentalist fat of the last fifty years with the deft touch of a surgeon and the encyclopedic knowledge of a veteran. Keep this book on your shelf. It will be an important reference for years to come.

– Greg Bishop

Acknowledgments

Many people have assisted in and supported my writing *The Cryptoterrestrials*, but a few stand out as particularly gracious and encouraging. In no particular order:

Elan Levitan
Nick Redfern
Paul Kimball
David Biedny and Gene Steinberg
Greg Bishop
Patrick Huyghe
William Michael Mott
"Mr. Ecks"
Michael Garrett

And, of course, everyone who's taken the time to comment on my weblog, *Posthuman Blues*.

Bibliography

Colin Bennett, *Looking for Orthon* (Paraview Press, 2001)

Marc Davenport, *Visitors from Time* (Greenleaf Publications, 1994)

Richard Dolan, *UFOs and the National Security State* (Keyhole Publishing, 2000)

John Fuller, *The Interrupted Journey* (Souvenir Press Ltd.)

Timothy Good, *Alien Base* (Harper Perennial, 1999)

Budd Hopkins, *Intruders* (Ballantine Books, 1997)

Budd Hopkins and Carol Rainey, *Sight Unseen* (Pocket Star, 2004)

Patrick Huyghe, *The Field Guide to Extraterrestrials* (Avon Books, 1996)

David Jacobs, *Secret Life* (Touchstone, 1993)

John Keel, *The Complete Guide to Mysterious Beings* (Tor Books, 2002)

John Keel, *The Eighth Tower* (Signet, 1977)

John Keel, *The Mothman Prophecies* (Tor Books, 2002)

John Mack, *Abduction* (Ballantine Books, 1997)

Ivan Sanderson, *Invisible Residents* (Adventures Unlimited Press, 2005)

Ivan Sanderson, *Uninvited Visitors* (Spearman, 1969)

Whitley Strieber, *Communion* (Avon, 1988)

Richard Thompson, *Alien Indentities* (Govardhan Hill, 1995)

Jacques Vallee, *The Invisible College* (Dutton, 1975)

Jacques Vallee, *Dimensions* (Ballantine Books, 1989)

R.A. Wilson, *Cosmic Trigger* (New Falcon Publications, 1991)

About the Author

Mac Tonnies (1975-2009) was an author and blogger whose work focused on futurology, transhumanism, and the paranormal. Tonnies grew up in Independence, Missouri. He was the author of two other books, a collection of science fiction short stories entitled *Illumined Black*, and *After the Martian Apocalypse*, an examination of the anomalies on the surface of Mars. His popular blog was called Posthuman Blues. Tonnies died at the age of 34 in Kansas City, Missouri.

Made in the USA
Middletown, DE
27 November 2023

43602423R00071